Who Will Reme

# Who Will Remember Me?

*A Daughter's Memoir of Grief and Recovery*

Barbara Hamilton-Holway

SKINNER HOUSE BOOKS
BOSTON

Printed in Canada.

Cover design by Kimberly Glyder.
Text design by Suzanne Morgan.

ISBN 1-55896-460-6

Library of Congress Cataloging-in-Publication Data

Hamilton-Holway, Barbara.
    Who will remember me? : a daughter's memoir of grief and recovery/
    Barbara Hamilton-Holway.
        p.cm.
    ISBN 1-55896-460-6 (alk. paper)
        1. Hamilton-Holway, Barbara. 2. Christian biography—United States.
    3. Bereavement—Religious aspects—Christianity. I. Title.

    BR 1725.H2338A3 2004
    248.8'66'092—dc21
    [B]                                                    2003052644

10 9 8 7 6 5 4 3 2
06 05 04

With love and gratitude to H. Bruce Hamilton and Marilyn Guerrieri; Lindsey Shea, Ashley Logan, Patty, and Alfred Charles Hamilton; Sarah Elizabeth Bush; Benjamin Hamilton Bush; Bill Hamilton-Holway; family; and friends. And with heartfelt thanks to the good people of the Unitarian Universalist Church of Berkeley, who granted me sabbatical leave, giving me time to reflect and write about my mother's living and dying.

*In memory of Gladys Hile Hamilton
and Charles Murray Hamilton.*

# Contents

# *Preface*

IN SEPTEMBER MY MOTHER DIED.

On a cross-country flight after her death, I got to talking with the man seated next to me, a retired medical doctor who now volunteers as a hospice companion. He said, "At the end of life, people wonder, 'Who will remember me?'"

Surely my mother wondered about who and how she would be remembered. Facing her death, I wonder, "Now who will remember me as a baby, as a girl, as a young woman?"

This is the story of my relationship with my mother, a story of both separation and connection. Much of what I know about love and power has come from my relationship with my mother. This relationship is the source of my first learning of good and evil, of survival, of love. In sharing the story of my own life—as a daughter, a mother, and a parish minister—I hope to convey my sense of an abiding relationship, a presence known by many names and no name, which some call God.

I have arranged the story in three parts: the events of diagnosis, illness, and death, followed by my effort to understand and accept this most unique and complicated of relationships, and finally, my search for the meaning that loss gives to life, that death gives to the living.

My mother is gone now, yet her profound effect on my life continues. In endings, as in beginnings, there is still relationship. In reading my story, I hope you will find your own meaning and grow in your understanding of the relationships that form and fill your life.

*I have come to bring you bitter news.*

—1 KINGS 14:6

MY MOTHER STANDS NAKED BEFORE ME.

Mother asked me to come into her motel bathroom. She has taken off her nightgown and is showing me her body. It is covered everywhere—head to toes—with red, swollen, itchy blotches.

Ten months ago my husband Bill and I moved from Utah to California. Our daughter Sarah, a college student, and our son Ben stayed in Utah. Now we have all gathered again in Salt Lake City for Ben's high school graduation. My parents have come from their home in Nebraska to celebrate with us.

The last time I had seen my parents was when they came to Bill's and my installation as the co-ministers of the Unitarian

Universalist Church of Berkeley. All the months between then and now, Mother has had a lingering cough. She told herself it was the last stage of a cold that she couldn't shake, but she finally got herself to the doctor. Before she left Nebraska for Utah, the doctor had her take a series of medical exams.

As Mother now stands before me, naked and disfigured, a roar rises up, shaking the motel.

All my life my mother has been so strong; it doesn't occur to me to rush her off to the emergency room. My brother Bruce and I have always predicted that she will outlive our father by decades. Our father Charlie was hospitalized for two years when we were children. He has an ileostomy and has worn an appliance in place of a colon for more years than he hasn't. He has had heart attacks and a hip replacement. Although his spirit is healthy, gentle, and strong, his body is weak.

Instead of taking Mother to the emergency room, I go out to a drugstore to buy her some anti-itch cream. The night is booming with police sirens and shouting, the streets are an obstacle course of speeding drunk drivers, and the sky is a chaos of strobe lights and fireworks. Everything seems garish and out of control. All of Salt Lake City is one resounding scream, a carousing riot—the Utah Jazz has won the National Basketball Association division title.

The next day Mother flies home to Nebraska and reports to her doctor. He sends her directly to the hospital. It turns out Mother was allergic to the barium she took for the MRI and X-ray exams before going to Utah. Her doctor brings in a specialist, and the two of them are shocked at the fluid that has built up in her lungs. Immediately, they drain two liters of fluid. This is no lingering cold.

The pulmonary specialist tells Mother she has late-stage lung cancer. Mother has never smoked and has lived all her life in Nebraska, whose state slogan is "the good life." She has lived under a big, open sky—not in industry and pollution but in clean air, farmland, and prairie.

Mother asks what this diagnosis means and then clarifies, directly asking how long she has to live. The pulmonary specialist says that based on her knowledge and experience, she would estimate four months. Boom. Our whole world is shaking.

NINE MONTHS AFTER MY MOTHER was diagnosed with lung cancer, we celebrate her eightieth birthday. I worship with her, my father, and my brother at our parents' church, the church of my childhood—First Plymouth Congregational Church, United Church of Christ, in Lincoln, Nebraska. As a minister, I find it humbling to sit in the congregation and take in a sermon by the senior minister and then hear what my family has to say about it afterward. My brother comments on how big the preacher's nose has become.

My brother and I have come from California for Mother's birthday. This is the first time in maybe thirty years that just the four of us, with no partners or grandchildren, have sat together around the dining room table. My brother and I and all our family have written tributes in celebration of Mother. Her children and grandchildren have written thanks:

> Thank you for the love between parents, love for better or for worse, in sickness and in health.

> Thank you for commitment, companionship, loyalty, love, and perseverance.

> Thank you for shared meals and good fun, for support, for hard work.

> Thank you for annual rituals—picnics, homemade ice cream, reunions, family across the generations.

> Thank you for golf and dancing, neighborhood walks, bike rides, badminton, swimming, tennis, catch, for all the cards and games and late-night laughter.

> Thank you for drawing and reading and playing with children; for homemade noodles; for fresh, warm homemade bread; for baking everyone their favorite

foods, especially desserts—pies, cakes, fudge, oatmeal raisin cookies, and the best chocolate chip cookies ever.

Thank you for family vacations and travel. Thank you for visits to Fiji, Arizona, Utah, and California; for the shared celebrations of graduations, ordination, weddings, birthdays, and holidays; and for sharing, as Charlie always says, "beautiful, great to be alive" days.

Thank you for a grandmother and granddaughter sharing getting their ears pierced.

Thank you for the cleanest, freshest-smelling clothes on the planet.

Thank you for explanations of world events and honestly spoken feelings about family events.

Thank you for all the thoughtfully chosen gifts, all the cards and letters.

Thank you for a circle of support at Charlie's bedside, hands held, hearts spoken.

Thank you for values taught through actions and reactions to the cards life has dealt you.

Thank you for strength, for talking through hard things, for speaking your mind, for hard work, for appreciation spoken, for unending support, for an indestructible faith in family.

Thank you for a pew shared at First Plymouth, for singing and music.

Thank you for all the love.

Fluid is building up around Mother's lungs, and it is hard for her to breathe—tiring, exhausting, draining, depleting. When Mother sees the photographs of the birthday celebration, she says she looked like death warmed over. My brother held back some of the photos because he thought they would only depress her. She looks like she is dying.

My mother has lived eighty years, outlived by five months her doctor's prognosis; been in a loving relationship with her husband for over fifty-seven years, and recently celebrated the announcement of the birth of Lindsey Shea, her first great-grandbaby. A blessed, full life. Still, she is my mother, and her dying breaks my heart.

A YEAR LATER, Mother is receiving chemotherapy for lung cancer. She has also been falling, possibly suffering small strokes. At the hospital where they have volunteered for many years, my parents go to a rehab group. The group keeps them socializing, as well as exercising. Most days they go, but some days Mother doesn't have the energy to stand up, bathe, or get dressed.

Sarah and I are here in Nebraska to help out and to celebrate another birthday—Mother's eighty-first. Mother has now outlived her four-month prognosis by twenty-one months.

My parents show us a video of Lindsey Shea, their first great-grandchild, taking her first steps. My father says, "You come into the world vulnerable, and you go out vulnerable."

You come into the world without possessions, and you go without possessions. As they weigh whether to stay in their longtime home or move to a retirement home, which would no doubt be my mother's last home, my parents are letting go of some of their things. Our days are spent going through cupboards, drawers, closets, and boxes in the house. We find a box of all the letters my father sent my mother during World War II, a box of cards they were sent when I was born, another box of letters my grandmother Ella Sophia treasured. We sort piles of photographs. Recognizing ourselves in one another, we three generations of women get laughing when we come to an overflowing, chaotic folder of papers labeled "Papers to Be Filed in the Proper Place."

On Mother's birthday, she has a good day. We let go of her hats. We take hatboxes filled with golf visors, garden hats, and Sunday dress hats to the rehab group and hand them out to everyone. Each man and woman on every stationary bike, Nordic track, or rowing machine is wearing a felt, fancy, straw, or billed hat. A big, burly guy peddles along, wearing a floppy pink hat with its sash flying.

But even on her good days, Mother is not the person she has always been. She has always been capable, hardworking, able to hold together many details. Her vitality, strong opinions and judgments, sharpness, concentration, and retention are fading.

When I am in my old bed in my parents' house, I stay awake nights thinking of my parents and their lives, what they are going through. I wonder what is ahead. Wasn't it just a short time ago that they were helping me move into my first home?

SARAH AND I HAVE EACH RETURNED to our homes after our visit to Nebraska. Sarah calls me, sobbing. On our visit, she was calm, strong, comforting, and thoughtful about all she was witnessing, and now she is beginning to feel. I want to be calming, comforting, strong for her. I tell her that we will always have our mother and grandmother. Nothing can take away her presence in our lives. Her influence, her impression, her love will go on and on. How could she not be among us?

I hang up the phone and cry.

We learn mother has had another small stroke. It's only a day after our visit, and she is in the hospital. How can I not be there helping my parents? How can I not be among them?

On the phone, Mother says, "Stay where you are. Enjoy Bill. Enjoy your home. Live your life." Mother tells me that no matter what happens, they will be all right.

I try to put my faith in that. If they heal and enjoy more years together, they will be all right. If one outlives the other by some years, they will be all right. When they die, they will be all right.

Mother says she and my father have no doubt of our love for them. We are with them always. We cannot *not* be among them.

❖

AFTER MOTHER'S LAST STROKE, it is finally crystal clear to all of us that my parents can no longer manage in their much-loved home. My brother Bruce and I return to Lincoln to move my parents from their longtime home to an apartment in a nearby retirement home. We choose items for the new apartment from among a big house full of furniture, and our father makes the move. Mother has been in a nursing home since she was discharged from the hospital.

Bruce spends the nights in their longtime home, and I stay in the second bedroom of my parents' new three-room apartment in the retirement home. My father goes to bed early, and each evening I drive back to their home. Although we all have been slowly going through their accumulation of a lifetime, there is still more. My parents have not only boxes of things they have saved, they have boxes of things my grandmother saved. Tokens of special times, kept for some always-future date to examine, to linger over, and to bring back memories, haven't been out of their boxes in decades. At night my brother and I have to take boxes and boxes of treasures, saved tokens and memorabilia, photographs and slides out to dump in the trash.

"We've got to learn from this, Barb. I'm serious. If I buy one book, I'm going to let go of two," says my brother.

"I've got to go home and sort through all the papers in the study, get rid of stuff boxed up in the basement and the garage," I say, as we vow to do things differently.

Mother has been very identified with her home, and it is not a place she wants to leave. We want to get paintings and photographs on the walls of the new apartment and make the place look as much like home as we can. When Mother leaves the nursing home, we want her to be surrounded by things that are lovingly familiar. We want her to feel like she is coming home.

The retirement home is not home. It has an institutional feel, an old-folks'-home feel. It has kitschy knickknacks, cheery decorations, and artificial flowers in the hallways and on the tables in the dining hall. The retirement home has a battalion of walkers. Half the people use walkers, all decorated with the same floral-print aprons tied around the silver-sheened handlebars to carry personal items like mail and keys. Some handlebars are decked out with bike bells, horns, and rearview mirrors. These people are trying too hard to have a good time.

Ten minutes before mealtime, like horses at the starting gate, everyone lines up at the dining hall doors waiting for the signal to enter. The bell rings, and people take their assigned seats and then wait again for their tables to get called to the buffet line. There they pick up their plastic trays and choose among the bedpan-style warmer trays of thrice-cooked meat and vegetables. All this anticipation for chipped beef on toast, limp broccoli, iceberg lettuce with cottage cheese, and wiggling red Jello cubes.

Many residents can't hear, so there's little conversation at the tables. Everyone seems much worse off than my parents. Are they really ready for this?

Each time my father and I arrive at the dining hall, the sound of the walkers crossing the floor halts. Everybody stops and looks up, checking us out. We are clearly the excitement and the talk of the place. We are creating quite a stir among the residents, because people are saying a new guy moved in with a much younger wife.

After we get Mother moved in and get to know people, one woman tells me with a wink, "I knew all along you were the daughter." Once Mother is moved in, she's relieved to be out of the nursing home and to be with my father. She is truly grateful for their new apartment, and she says, "I'm glad to be home."

◈

I'VE WATCHED HOME MOVIES of my mother, filmed in the 1940s and 1950s. Although my parents weren't rich, Mother took good care of clothing, made things last, and appeared beautiful and stylish. On a 1957 trip to Hollywood, in her swimsuit and sunglasses, she looked like a star.

On her eighty-first birthday, when she was weak and sick, she was still glad to receive a new crinkly skirt, knit top, and blazer. She mustered the energy to try it all on, and for a few minutes she and my father took each other in their arms and danced.

By the next month she had let go of her home and furnishings, her dress-up clothes, and her dancing shoes, and my parents had made the move to a retirement home. Now, not very many months later, her clothes have to be changed several times a day, always with the challenge of finding shirts and pants that aren't stained. Soon she is arriving at the dining hall in elastic waist–banded clothing with her catheter showing.

A series of small strokes has made it hard for her to learn again to walk, to care for herself, to remember the name of her first great-grandchild. The little notes and word games she left around to help exercise her mind don't matter anymore. Her handwriting has always been beautiful, and now she can barely sign her name to medical forms.

Throughout her life, Mother always played games, cards, and dominoes. She played well, with gusto and humor. The games were always full of laughter. (There is the family story, though, of a time when my parents were vacationing at a cottage. My father won so many hands of cards that Mother threw the whole deck in the lake.) When we visit my parents, we try to reclaim this way we all have had of being together, but it is hard. Mother cannot hold the cards. We try something else. We play what will be her last game. She puts much effort into handling the dominoes and focusing her mind on the numbers and the rules. We, her family, watch her struggling and feel grief and sorrow, tenderness and affection.

We watch her suffer. Lung cancer makes her breathing labored, her cough constant. The effort to push herself up out of the wheelchair or to do any ordinary personal care, such as bathing herself or brushing her teeth, is enormous and often unsuccessful. Still, we see in her weakness also her great strength. And we watch her let go of everything. This once strong, powerful, capable, giving, and serving woman lets her husband, children, and grandchildren do for her. We witness her experience of loss, but also her experience of finding. She finds she can accept our care.

❖

OUR FAMILY CONTINUES to say goodbye to my mother. All my life my mother has been a mountain of strength. When she had her first fall, it was in a grocery store. Her feet flew out from under her and she slammed into the floor, catching most of her weight on her elbow. Hearing her slam onto the floor and scream in pain, people came running from all over the store to help her. She was embarrassed and uncomfortable with offers of assistance. Wanting to maintain her dignity, she said, "Is there anything I can get you while I'm down here?"

More falls happen, small strokes continue, and cancer cells multiply in her body. We watch this powerful woman grow weak and diminish before our disbelieving eyes.

Right after Bill and I leave from a visit, my parents are in the nursing station of the retirement home, and Mother falls again. The fall sends her back to the hospital. After some days in the hospital, she is moved again to a nursing home. Her time there is dreadful. I return to visit and sit with her for a meal in the dining area of the nursing home's stroke section. The patients around her are moaning, groaning, drooling, or vacant. I am full of sorrow, full of compassion. I try to offer respect and show regard for the other patients. I try to be present to Mother, try to make a good dinnertime together. Mother says, "When you've been through everything I've been through, you know there are things worse than death."

There is so much suffering. My mother is suffering.

As I MAKE VISITS to my parents in Nebraska, I'm a little mixed up about the word *home*. As I leave California, I say, "I'm going away from home." When I say where I'm going, I say, "I'm going home to Nebraska to visit my folks." Of course, my folks are no longer in their home. They have moved into a retirement home, and currently Mother is back as a patient in a nursing home.

Even when I am in my own home, I sometimes find myself saying, "I just want to go home." I want to go home to where I am accepted, where I am loved. I want to be in the place where everything is going to be all right. Sometimes I am homesick for myself—homesick for who I know I want to be, can be, really am.

In my childhood, though my parents worked together both at home and at their hardware store, I thought of these places as *my father's store* and *my mother's house*. At that time I believed that my mother's house was too narrow and confining; it didn't have room for the fullness of who I was.

For as long as I can remember I have had dreams of a big, old, wonderful house, full of great rooms and passageways. The house has more rooms than I first realize. In dreams, I think I am awake, and I believe my house really holds these additional rooms. I am excited and comforted as I think, "Oh, it turns out the dream really is true!"

In subsequent dreams, I can find my way into these secret inner rooms, really a house within a house. In my dreams, when I find I am in this familiar house, I am always glad.

Sometimes I notice healthy green plants in these inner rooms, and I know that when I'm not there, someone is taking care of everything. Sometimes I feel someone's presence, but I only barely catch a glimpse.

In some of my dreams, rather than just paying occasional visits, I am living in the house all the time. Living there continually, I feel encouraged to do what I need to do without worry that I'd better be careful or I'll be out of a job and out of a house. I can risk being myself. I have a home where I can always go.

Mother, in the nursing home, begins to say in phone calls that she wants to go home. She's not clear if she means she wants to go home to their home of thirty-five years, or to her apartment with my father in the retirement home, or somewhere else. Sometimes she says, "I want to be called home." Mother wants to go home to where she is accepted, where she is loved, where everything is going to be all right. Mother wants to go to a place she half-remembers, half-imagines—a place where she doesn't have to worry, where she will always be welcomed home.

"Home," wrote Emily Dickinson, "is the definition of God." And, as the gospel hymn "Amazing Grace" sings, "grace will lead me home."

I CALL MOTHER. She has been released from the nursing home and has returned to the retirement home, but she is confused about where I now live and where she is. She tells me, "I'm where they put cranky old women." She says, "I guess it's just okay to toss mothers aside like a piece of trash." I listen. I try to be present. I try to acknowledge how hard it must be for her. She mocks my comments. She mocks me. She says, "It's obvious what mothers are worth—nothing."

My father takes the phone from her and says, "I'm sorry. She doesn't mean that." He's right. In the big picture, Mother means it when she says, "I feel your love. I'm sending love right back to you." She means it when she says, "Stay right where you are. Live your life." But it is also true that Mother feels worthless, discarded, left, lost, forsaken.

I think about how she sounded on one of my recent visits — bitter, mistrusting of my father. Three times a day he pushes her wheelchair to the dining hall, carrying her walker. Their room is as far from the dining room as anyone can be in this retirement home. This man, who has stents placed in his arteries to hold them open, who is weak, and who everyone thought was going to die first, patiently lifts Mother out of her wheelchair. He helps her walk—oh, so slowly—teetering into the dining room with her walker. This is a retirement home, not a nursing home. There are rules about not coming into the dining hall in a wheelchair. On this visit, Charlie was his regular, friendly self, greeting each person they passed. As he greeted a woman, my mother said to me out of the side of her mouth, "That's his girlfriend."

Mother feels alone and abandoned.

I went with Mother to the retirement home's exercise class, where she tried to participate as best she could from her wheelchair. We stayed for the current events class that follows exercise. The activity leader raised for discussion a news arti-cle about a city ordinance requiring homeowners to control their dogs. The leader asked, "When a dog is barking at night, what do you ladies think should be done?" Several women, former schoolteachers themselves, responded to each of the leader's questions by raising their hands. They were eager to please. No matter how obvious the answer, they were eager to give it. Mother said under her breath, but so I could hear, "Shoot it." I had to hold in my laughter, and she loved that. When the leader asked, "I know you ladies like fresh fruit and candy, but is there anything else you would like me to pick up as awards for the winners of this afternoon's bingo game?" Mother said, again under her breath, "Yeah, a bottle of wine."

Even though Mother is losing her mental awareness and alertness, she is not willing to be patronized. She will not become a child back in school, pleasing a teacher. She is holding onto the ways she has always had of being true to herself. And the truth she does not hide on our phone call is her despair.

WE ARE ALWAYS SAYING HELLO and goodbye in this world. Each transition is partly an arrival, partly a departure, always a kind of commencement. The wheel of life keeps on turning.

I remember when I saw my daughter off to her first day as a seventh grader in a small, experimental junior high program in a large high school. We agreed that we would walk together to her bus stop and that when the bus came into sight, I'd leave. When we got near the bus stop, I could see all the big high school students standing and waiting. I said to Sarah, "You probably want me to go now." We said goodbye. I hid behind a van to watch.

A very crowded bus arrived. All the big kids and Sarah boarded. Sarah's world was expanding. I wondered if she, like me, was remembering the stories that seventh graders hear about older kids initiating new ones. I thought of the poet Netta Gillespie's words: "I hurl you into the universe and pray."

An older couple came walking down the sidewalk. They must have wondered what I was doing hiding behind a van. As they approached, the woman said, "Seeing your kids off on their first day of school?" They had seen it all before. For this is our human story—of letting go, of endings and beginnings, of departures and arrivals, of venturing forth and coming home.

It is fall, and Bill and I are putting our twenty-year-old son Ben on a train headed east, the beginning of his cross-country adventure. He's taking time off from college to see the country, visit other schools, work on a communal farm, discover himself. His world is expanding. We send him off with bread and cheese, with fruit and cookies, with joyous wishes and tears, with a hurl into the universe and a prayer.

At the same time, I am saying goodbye to my mother. Her world has diminished from the whole planet to the United States to Nebraska to Lincoln to her neighborhood to her home to her retirement home.

Sometimes I have an image of my mother from a time in my late teens and early twenties. She is strong, powerful, full of life, talking, laughing. And it seems like such a short time ago. At my lowest, I think, What's the point? At my best, I think, How do we fully, gratefully, lovingly live our days, which seem so brief right now?

My father keeps on. He cares for Mother and continues to volunteer at the hospital. He goes regularly to an exercise class. He tells me that it is sometimes hard to get himself there and get himself going, but once he does he is always glad. He goes to the dining hall. He greets everyone by name. He jokes with the nurses and aides, slips them candy bars, thanks them. Residents of the retirement home love him. He cries as he tells me that someone slipped a loving, supportive note under his door this morning.

The wheel keeps on turning. This fall we are saying good-bye to my mother; we release her into the universe and pray.

I AM A MINISTER needing a minister. As my mother's world is diminishing from home to retirement home to one room, I am falling apart.

Mother's clothes are stained and need to be washed; her drawstring pants are too loose and too long, and they need to be tightened and hemmed. Her bedding is wet, her diaper needs changing, and surely a bath and a shampoo would feel good. There are exercises she's supposed to do, but it is such an effort just to get her up and out of the bed. There are still more possessions to sort through and photograph albums to show her. There are letters to write to family and phone calls to return. There are insurance forms to understand and conversations we haven't had.

Mother's minister, the Reverend Kathryn Campbell, steps into the chaos and speaks a prayer, naming what is going on. She doesn't demonstrate her knowledge; she doesn't socialize; she doesn't linger. This visit is not about her. She steps in, speaks, touches, moves on. She is a solid, peaceful presence, a face and voice of love.

When Moses was born, it was into chaos. The pharaoh had ordered the murder of Hebrew infants. All hell was breaking loose. Moses' parents hid their baby for three months, and when they could no longer keep him hidden, they released him to the river to take a chance, the slim chance, of his survival. When Moses was drawn forth from the water by the pharaoh's daughter, his sister Miriam, who had been watching and waiting, stepped forward. Miriam offered to find a nursemaid for the boy, and she brought her own mother to the pharaoh's daughter. And so, in the pharaoh's palace, Moses continued to be nurtured and loved by his own mother. Through Miriam's presence and action, Moses maintained his Hebrew heritage, which strengthened him to become the one who could lead the people out of slavery and into freedom. Miriam's ministry slipped in at the right moment, and her small contribution made a big difference. Her action set in motion the chain of events that would lead to the freeing of captives and the journey to the promised land. Life depends on Miriams.

In Kathryn's presence, I take a deep breath. I'm reminded of what's most important. In the moment I feel steadied and grounded. I can continue, simply doing one thing at a time. If Mother and I never look at the album, it will be okay. If the clothes don't get altered, if the exercises are left undone, it will be okay. In this foreign world of the retirement home, in this world of our family turned upside down, I'm doing what I can, when I can, to nurse and nurture and love my own mother.

Kathryn's presence restores my faith. In the midst of chaos, grief, and loss, I'm not alone. Each family member is stepping forward. Each one of us is doing what he or she can. Each becomes the face and voice and hands of love. I put my trust in this love. Like Miriam, like Kathryn, each of us steps forward, offering a simple, single action that ministers and makes all the difference.

ON HIS CROSS-COUNTRY TRIP, Ben spends five days with his grandparents. Mother has hospice care now in her room at the retirement home. She no longer goes to the dining hall for meals. She's confined to her bed and is in hospital gowns day and night. She eats and speaks very little; mostly she sleeps.

Mother tells Ben she is hungry for strawberries. She is no longer able to pull forward her past and speak of it. Ben crawls right in bed with his Grams, holds her, feeds her strawberries and memories. "Remember when you showed up at my school? You'd just come for a visit, and I hadn't seen you yet. You stood right in front of me. I was an introverted first grader, off in my own little world, walking down the hallway, staring at my shoes, so out of it that I didn't see you. I moved aside. You kept blocking me, and I kept moving. I moved, you moved. I moved, you moved. We were doing a little dance, a kind of fox-trot, our feet meeting toe to toe. *Finally* I looked up. I was so happy to see you! I remember laughing and laughing."

"I remember," Grams says.

"Remember," Ben says, as he feeds his grandmother another bite of strawberry, "when you were visiting us, and you put bubble bath in the tub and put the jets on? Bubbles filled the tub and the shower stall so you couldn't open the doors. You were drowning in bubbles. You howled. All the way upstairs, we could hear you laughing."

"I'll never forget," Grams says.

I think about the Buddhist story of the man hanging over the edge of the cliff, with a tiger chasing after him, mice chewing away at the vine that the man grasps with one hand while the other hand reaches for a strawberry. Mother has cancer spreading in her body, strokes that have diminished her physically and mentally, and falls that have set her back. And her grandson feeds her strawberries and memories. Oh, how sweet those strawberries!

THE TIME IS COMING to say a last goodbye. It is mid-September. Nearly twenty-seven months have passed since Mother was diagnosed with late-stage lung cancer. But when is the time? I have a flight scheduled in a week, but will that be too late? Should I fly now?

Bruce arrives in Lincoln on Wednesday. He sits by Mother, quietly holding her hand. It is late for her. He asks, "Are you tired? Do you want to go to sleep?"

She says sweetly, "I have company."

Nurses tell Bruce that Mother seems to have improved some the last day or two. I decide to wait.

On Thursday morning, the hospice nurse calls and tells me I had better come. Sarah and I fly out immediately. When we arrive in Lincoln, Mother's world has shrunk from one room to one bed to one more breath. She is working hard to breathe, her eyes are glassed over and unfocused, she is running a fever, she seems far away. When Sarah says, "Grams," that seems to call her. Mother softly repeats, "Grams." And when I say, "Sarah and I are here," she says, "Barb." She knows both Sarah and I are with her, and she says to us, "I love you."

Friday, she continues to work hard to breathe, and she barely speaks. Breathing takes all her strength. Once when the phone rings, though, she says, "That phone's always waking me up!" She doesn't talk much after that, but we talk to her. We invite her to relax, want her to feel peace, thank her for working hard all her life, and tell her she can let go now. We tell her we will always love her, always miss her, always be grateful to her—but that we will be okay, that we will love each other. Sarah and I sing to her: "Too-ra-loo-ra-loo-ra: An Irish Lullaby," "All through the Night," and "Like a Mother and Child." My father, Bruce, Sarah, and I, our faces showing love, encircle Mother's bed, holding her hands, head, and feet. I feel the presence of the rest of the family there with us.

Earlier in the month, Bruce brought his partner Marilyn for a visit. Mother had not met Marilyn before, and she said, "I really love her." During the summer, my nephew Alfie and his wife Patty also visited. Mother, who used to worry that none of her grandchildren would have children, met and held her first great-grandchild. When Bill and I visited later that month, a musical group came to the retirement home and played the piano and sang 1940s songs. Mother's foot was tapping, and her face was joyful. Just days before, Ben had had a good five-day visit.

In the last months of Mother's life, every time I would tell her we all loved her, she said she could feel the love. She told me she was not scared, was not worried, and was not in pain.

Mother labors to breathe. She sleeps fitfully. Charlie whispers to us, "There comes a time, don't you think, when rather than continuing to struggle, you would just want to let go?"

We decide to go to bed, and she seems much calmer and quieter when we leave her bedside. Our desire to have her still with us was making her hold on. Still, we hold her in our love all through the night. Bruce is with her again at two in the morning. Then, at four in the morning, when all of us are asleep, Mother takes her last breath.

BRUCE WAKES SARAH and me to tell us Mother has died. We hold one another and cry. Charlie, Bruce, Sarah, and I take our places again around the hospital bed and hold Mother. We sit beside her and read aloud the tributes all the family members wrote to her on her eightieth birthday, and we say goodbye.

The hospice nurse arrives to be with us. A man from the mortuary takes Mother's body from the bed. We hold one another and cry.

On Saturday our minister Kathryn sits and talks with us about the marking events in Mother's life and what we want in the service. Alfie, Ben, and Bill all fly into town. On Sunday the family goes to church, where Kathryn holds our family in her prayer. The Sunday service includes the singing of Brian Wren's hymn "Bring Many Names." The verses on "strong Mother God" and "warm Father God" have us all weeping.

❖

WE BUSY OURSELVES. Sarah, Ben, and I make photo boards for Mother's service that will show photographs of her with family and friends throughout her life. Bruce organizes the family for pie tasting at various bakeries around town. Mother made some of the best pies around, and in her honor, we want to offer all who gather for the service a reception of really good pie and the sharing of memories.

A few years back, Ben made a video interviewing Grams and Gramps, and we all watch it. We have recently gotten all the old home movies onto video, and we watch them, too. Bruce and Alfie get so much done at the retirement home; they move Charlie into a one-room apartment.

The phone calls of friends and relatives across the country and the presence of friends stepping in and helping or just being a supportive presence make all the difference.

Flowers, cards, poems, little gifts, and e-mail messages from colleagues and church members are meaningful. What a difference people's care makes!

At the service, we are all moved by the number of relatives, neighbors, and friends from throughout my mother's and father's lives who have come. Charlie—what an amazing man he is—has energy and gentle strength as he greets everyone and is appreciative, friendly, loving, giving, courageous.

Months before my parents moved from home to retirement home, Bruce and I were going through things in Mother's kitchen. Among her handwritten lists of memory tests, names of people important to her, and vocabulary words, we found a page where Mother had written down the people, events, experiences, and values that she had held dear in her life. On this page she also had written a list of favorite music, songs to which she and my father had loved to dance: "Rhapsody in Blue," "The Way We Were," "Unforgettable" with Nat King Cole and Natalie Cole, Frank Sinatra singing "All the Way" and "Softly, As I Leave You," and Glen Miller's "Stardust." Clearly, the lists were thoughts and music to select among for her memorial service.

Bruce took the list home and made a tape of music. As Mother was dying, the tape was playing. Mother spoke some of her last words: "Go with that one." She knew she was dying, and she was saying yes to the song as one for her funeral. A hymn we sing at church on Easter Sunday celebrates the Easter message as "Change then mourning into praise, and for dirges, anthems raise." Mother chose not dirges but dance songs.

Sitting in the chapel at the service for Mother, we listen to the music. Kathryn leads a beautiful service celebrating Mother's life. On this sunny, blue-sky clear day at a cemetery outside of town, near the graves of Mother's parents, two brothers, and sister, we bury Mother.

*I am with you always.*

—MATTHEW 28:20

WHAT'S THE POINT?

The last two years of her life, my mother let go of all the things she had cared so deeply about and worked so hard to maintain: her home, her mind, her independence. As a woman who grew up during the Great Depression, she made purchases wisely and took care of her things to make them last. When she moved with my father to a small space in a retirement home with no family nearby, Mother's carefully tended and cherished things brought in a few dollars in a rummage sale, and much went the way of the trash. This powerful, strong woman weakened, diminished, suffered, and died. What difference did her life make? What is the point of living?

I went from Mother's death right back to the busyness of church life and ministry. Now on sabbatical, I leave home, church, and city and head for the desert.

"Can God spread a table in the desert?" asks Psalm 78. How does healing come after pain and despair? How does the desert bloom? What kind of readying and labor prepares the way for life? Can readying yourself, rising out of bed, greeting the day with gratitude, smoothing down the sheets, making the bed, dressing, and showing up prepare the way? Can laying out a clean, ironed cloth on the table, arranging flowers, polishing the chalice, and lighting candles make the way for life?

The Israelites wandered in the wilderness. They left their homes, their familiar surroundings, and everything that had been certain. They had a longing for something else, for something more. They spent forty years searching for the promised land, their skin burned by the sun, sand, and wind, and the desert dust in their eyes, ears, teeth, and hair. Wandering around in circles for forty years, the Israelites had to have asked themselves, What's the point?

Moses told the people they were to make a tent, an ark, a wooden table, a tabernacle with curtains of fine linens, and an altar. They were to take sweet spices to make incense, prepare a lamp stand, and be ready with oils for the light. They were to carry all this around with them through all their days in the wilderness—always ready.

In the desert of Southern California, I move into the Sisters of the Company of Mary's Vina De Lestonnac Convent. In the private study that the sisters provide is a bare table, a chair. I turn the table to face the window and a whiteboard. I reach into my bag and pull out sharpened pencils, pens, and paper. I set up my computer. On the whiteboard I write some lines of my favorite scriptures. I set before me lines of poetry.

I place on the table the candle that my congregation has sent with me. I prepare the way. I turn on the computer, open a new file, and write, "In September my mother died."

❖

I AM BEGINNING my eighteen days in the desert at a Catholic convent and retreat center. I am walking the neighboring vineyards and hills, remembering my mother. I am looking for signs from my mother, paying attention to little found objects and seeing what memories and reflections they evoke. I notice and pick up a long length of dark and shiny, narrow, curly ribbon.

In the beginning, a first home—my mother's womb, her body, my consecrated host. In her I lived and moved and had my being. Communion, intimate relationship, is our oldest and deepest knowing. We were one and became two, though sometimes I think the umbilical cord connecting my mother and me was never severed. Like a thin, dark ribbon, like a telephone line stretching from Nebraska to California, it grew thinner and thinner and longer and longer through the years, but it was never quite cut. Maybe even now it is a strand, almost invisible.

I nursed at her breast, and she quenched my thirst. She was the provider of my daily bread, many a banquet, many a feast. She refreshed my weariness. I found comfort in her arms, in the laying on of her hands. She bathed me, washed and cleansed my wounds. She could kiss it and make it all better. Mother—a god in the shape of a woman, a woman in the shape of a god.

I am a second child. My mother told me that before I was born she asked my father how she would be able to love another child when she loved my brother so much? And then she said, "Then there was Barb." She said she couldn't believe how much love she had to give.

Love took the form of washing the clothes. When I was young, my mother washed the clothes on a washboard and hung the clothes outdoors on the line. What a fresh, sweet smell! Long before the time she washed clothes for her grandchildren, she was using an electric washer and dryer. Still, my son remembers that hers was the cleanest-smelling laundry on the planet. Love took the form of her hand-embroidered pillowcases, which to this day still make me feel loved.

She was a kind of first aid station. Her kitchen was the heart of the home. She rocked me to sleep. She sang me songs like "An Irish Lullaby," "Galway Bay," and 1940s big band tunes. She carefully chose gifts for me. And she always had plenty of words, words, words.

How beautiful she looked dressed up to go to church or to go out dancing with my father, how she swam off with sure strokes, how she sang and played the piano, how gracefully she danced, how capable she was! Her embrace, her arms around me, was like a life preserver—or a straitjacket.

◈

MY BROTHER AND I were blessed and cursed to be the center of my mother's life, the center of her universe. I remember feeling it was a burden that my mother's life seemed so wrapped up in my own. I was angry that even when she worked outside the home, her children were her career. From my point of view, she overinvested in her children. Our successes and failures were not ours, but hers. I resented that she was quick to make a judgment and was nearly always right. She saw right through a lie, yet she saw the truth in the worst light. She could make me feel guilty when I didn't even know what I had done. How often I viewed her as judgmental, critical, negative.

Mothering smothering. Mother's love was creative and destructive at the same time. She was my slave, my master, my maid, my martyr, my playmate, my teacher, my critic, my cheerleader, my judge, and my defender: "You're getting kinda chubby, Barb. . . . Is that a pimple? . . . Have another piece of chocolate cake. . . . Want some chocolate chip cookies, some ice cream?" And there was the battle of the hair—how to manage, control, and tame my hair!

There seemed to me to be so many conditions to fulfill to earn her love. She was a monster in the shape of a woman, a woman in the shape of a monster.

I blamed her for my inadequacies. I could never do things up to her standards. There were tasks I never could seem to do right and tasks I never could get her to stop doing for me, so I just let her do them, and I put some distance between us. That kind of distance isn't healthy, freeing, or separating. The distance isn't real. Either presence or absence can be a blessing, and either can be a curse.

How can we love and relate, and not be fused? How can we be both separate and together? Even as a young girl, I had the fear of becoming my mother. I would look at my hands and think, "That's how Mother would hold hers." I'd change the position of my hands and then think, "That's exactly how Mother would change hers." My brother would say that our grandmother Ella Sophia, whom we called

Munga, was becoming just like our great-grandmother Johanna, and Mother was becoming like Munga. "Watch out, Barb," he'd say.

My power and passion come from separating from my mother and relating to her, accepting her weaknesses and strengths as her own and mine as my own. I want to know my own limitations and gifts. I want to see and be seen in wholeness, in uniqueness. I want a sense of self, nurtured in communion.

My friend Kerstin, when her son was young, would rise in the night to his cries. She would rock him and nurse him, reciting the words of Kahlil Gibran: "Your children are not your children. They come through you but are not you."

Just as my children are not my children, my mother is not my mother. I came through her, but she is not me. I am reminded of this—with joy. I delight in photos of my mother in her life before I was born. There Mother is a child with laced-up boots, swinging from a tire swing; a kid dressed in overalls, freckled and beaming, her arm around her best friend, her cousin; a youth waving from the running board of a model T Ford on a family vacation to Colorado; a young woman rowing a boat; a young woman playing tennis; a bride walking down the aisle arm in arm with my father; and Mother holding her infant son, my big brother.

I participate in my own creation and in the creation of my mother. We are co-creators of each other. In relationships, we are both the changer and the changed.

Separating, letting go—it doesn't come easy. When I was in the Peace Corps in the Fiji Islands, eighteen thousand miles from my mother, I felt her influence even more than when my room was next to hers in her house. When I was in graduate school, in seminary, my mother was visiting me. I was thirty-six years old. We were together, preparing a meal in the kitchen. She said to me, "Oh, Barbara, be careful with that knife." And I thought, "Who does she think reminds me when she's not here?" A moment passed, and I cut my finger with the knife. Her mothering continued. When I was fifty, she greeted me with, "I won't say for the millionth time, when are you going to get your hair cut?"

"No matter how old a mother is," writes Florida Scott-Maxwell, "she watches her middle-aged children for signs of improvement."

HERE AT THE CONVENT are images of Mary and Jesus, of mother and child. I am created in Mother's image. I am a mother.

I loved being pregnant. I was so obviously a part of something larger than myself. I was carrying creation as if encircling the whole globe inside me. I was carrying power within me. This power evoked fear and wonder. I did not really know what all this pregnancy would mean, what all it would demand, or what would unfold. I experienced this mysterious presence, and I responded with some fear and reservation, with much awe and anticipation.

Many Christmas Eve candlelight services during my ministry have included a blessing shared by two women of the Bible who were surprised to be pregnant, the old Elizabeth and the young Mary. Elizabeth would give birth to John the Baptist and Mary, to Jesus. The first year I pieced together the blessing with words from Walt Whitman, Eve Miriam, and the book of Luke woven together with my own words. I read the part of Mary, and my mother read the part of Elizabeth. In a few years, my daughter read Mary's part, and I read the part of Elizabeth. Mary's response to Elizabeth's blessing is, "My body, my soul mirrors, magnifies God. My spirit rejoices in creation."

Mothering joins the human and the divine. Remarkable changes happen, most obviously in the body. Here is creation, transformation; a baby forms in the womb. A mother spends nine months turning bread and wine into the body and blood of new life. Milk rises in the breasts; this body gives and sustains life without losing life. The human body both mirrors and magnifies divine creativity; the spirit rejoices in creation.

*Virgin mother* is not an oxymoron but rather my longed-for reality, virgin meaning being whole unto one's self and, at the same time, being a mother, intimately relating to another. I want images in paintings of Mary birthing Jesus—of that crowning moment. If depicting the Crucifixion, the crown of thorns, was not too much, why not the birth? I want images of Joseph wiping a bottom. I want art glorifying parenting.

Still, I am glad for all the artistic images of Mother and Child—of Mother holding her newborn; Mother in blues and clay reds, like intense blue sky and rich earth, with the crescent moon at her feet, her child sometimes holding a globe; images of Mother holding the lifeless body of her adult son. If she can hold that body, she can hold the whole world.

❖

MOTHERING HELPED ME mother myself. Driving so carefully home from the hospital with an infant, I was seeing the world as if for the first time. Everything was fresh, new, and beautiful, glowing, fragile, and precious. I beheld everything, and it was good.

I wanted to say yes to all this goodness, yes to my children. I didn't want to say "no, no, no" to them. I wanted to say "yes, yes, yes." I wanted to encourage their curiosity and exploration, provide a wide variety of experiences. I knew my children would get ideas from me on how people live, and so I more carefully, more consciously, chose how to live my life.

The sight of my children's blood made my body hurt. I wanted to protect them. Mothering helped me understand my own mother's protectiveness.

My children are not my children. They come through me but are not me. They are, as Kahlil Gibran christened them, "life's longing for itself." Can a mother, can my mother, can I ever get it right—find a balance of interest and attention and separation and distance?

I read these words of Matthew Fox years ago and continue to hold them close:

> What sort of a person would I be if someone had deprived me from my childhood right up to today of every skinned knee or hurt feeling each time I desired to jump literally or symbolically? Does this caution clothed in sympathy too often prevail and so prevent the experience of extremes and even of God? Why don't we let each other suffer the consequences of our desires and decisions? Who are we to say what is best or better for a person, as if being sheltered from hurt is always and every time the best thing?

In mothering my children, I gave myself room to explore and dare, and I said yes to me. Yes to my children, yes to myself. I opened to experiences, chancing even the experience of God.

AFTER MOTHER DIED, I looked in the family Bible, where Mother recorded births and deaths of family members. I found, tucked into the Bible, a couple of Ann Landers columns on daughters not appreciating their mothers until they were gone. When Mother clipped these columns, did she do so thinking of herself as a mother or as a daughter? I asked my father how Mother was after her mother's death. "Guilty," he said. "She felt guilty—you know, always wondering what more she could have done."

I remember Mother telling me that as a child, she believed her mother favored her older sister—the pretty one, the one who played the piano by ear, the vivacious one, the wilder one. Mother was more like the older child in the story of the prodigal son. She stayed close by her mother, was always involved in her life, cared for her as she aged. Mother's sister and living brother moved away, moved from thing to thing and person to person. Yet their infrequent calls and cards and attention to their mother were what my grandmother praised.

I remember my mother telling me, after her mother died, how hard her mother had worked and how she appreciated all she did—how she only then understood her. Maybe all Mother had wanted was for her mother to hold her face in her hands, kiss her forehead, and tell her she was blessed to be her mother.

I wonder what all the ways I've let my mother down are. Mother wanted me not to spill milk on the clean kitchen floor, not to go out in the cold without my overcoat buttoned up, not to go out in the wind without a scarf over my ears, and not to go out in the rain at all. She wanted me to marry and to stay married. She wanted me to respect hard work and cleanliness and to pass those values on to my children. She wanted me to get my hair cut. She was proud that I became a minister, but she would have liked it more if I had been ordained as a Congregationalist rather than a Unitarian Universalist.

But maybe not. Maybe all she wanted was for me to follow my heart and still open my heart to her for the choices she made. Maybe all she wanted was for me to hold her face in my hands, kiss her forehead, and tell her I was blessed to be her daughter.

I LOVE TAKING improvisational movement classes. They stretch me to give expression to my experiences and feelings.

In one class years ago, the teacher invited each of us to pick up a cloth and dance with it as if it were something precious to us. What was precious to me? My children. I cradled the cloth in my arms as my precious babies, but the babies became my father, whose life had been threatened by a heart attack and who was becoming weak and frail. I danced with the cloth, tears running down my face. I danced gratitude and grief, love and letting go.

Years later, when I was moving from Utah to California, Sarah and I went to a drop-in dance class. The teacher began the class by asking people what was going on in their lives. I said I was moving and was busy with all the work of a move. I said I was leaving one house that had not yet sold and was uncertain what house I was moving into. I said I was leaving a congregation I loved and a community and a land I had come to love. Then I said that I guessed what was weighing on my heart most was that I was moving and my children were not. I wouldn't be living with Sarah and Ben. The teacher said, "Dance that." She set out props, art implements, cloths, and scarves. Separately, Sarah and I danced with flowing white cloths. I danced near Sarah, my movements encouraging, upholding, and supporting her. While Sarah soared, I was sending energy and love toward her. I danced as if I were the breeze in her hair, the grass beneath her feet, the breath of life around her. I danced as if all that was good and wise and honest and beautiful was supporting Sarah.

At one point, Sarah's hand reached back and brushed my foot, and we began dancing together, wrapped in our two cloths. We were one and apart, holding and releasing, crying.

I folded my cloth—I remember thinking that it was like folding diapers. I didn't interrupt Sarah but quietly offered her the cloth, placing it nearby. She danced with it and made it part of her cloth. Then she took a card and wrote on it two mirrored images of the word *honor*, meeting in the center, barely touching. Sarah folded the two cloths and placed the card on them. We danced our dance of life—uniting and letting go.

OUT WALKING THE ACRES of the convent, I find another scrap of ribbon—this one a rainbow of colors.

"Why do you have to wear a necklace and flaunt your sexuality?" Mother once asked Sarah, her two fingers crooked in my daughter's necklace, twisting and turning it. "I don't have to wear a necklace that says, 'I'm straight,'" Mother said as she tightened her hold on the string around my daughter's neck and tugged again, sending the rainbow beads flying, clacking across the kitchen floor, rolling under ledges, hiding in little cracks.

That happened several years ago, before Mother's cancer, at Sarah's high school graduation. Her grandparents had traveled from Nebraska to Utah to attend the ceremonies. Beforehand, Sarah had written her grandparents a long letter in which she came out as lesbian. The visit was shaped by my mother's fears—fears for Sarah's life and well-being, fears of what she and my father would tell their friends, fears of what Sarah's being a lesbian meant about them and about me, their daughter. Mother's fear was sometimes a quiet, brooding anger and sometimes an explosive, wild rage. I didn't know until later that, earlier on this visit, a friend of mine who also wore a rainbow necklace told Mother that the necklace was a sign of gay pride. The build up of reading Sarah's letter and then seeing her necklace became just too much for Mother.

We all sat in the living room and tried to talk. We took my parents to the movie *Philadelphia*, and midway through it they walked out, crying.

Years passed, and significant parts of Sarah's life were just not discussed with her grandparents. She felt more and more distant from them—chatty and friendly, but unreal and disconnected.

Three Junes after Sarah's high school graduation, Mother was diagnosed with inoperable lung cancer. When Mother turned eighty years old and all the family sent her written tributes, Sarah named many wonderful shared memories in hers. She detailed the ways in which her grandmother, throughout her life, had given her love.

Sarah also spoke honestly and wrote,

I have vivid memories of the difficult feelings and conversations between us connected to my being lesbian, and the times since then when I've felt like there were joys in my life I couldn't share with you. I know you want the best for me. I am so appreciative of your consistent love and care and concern for my happiness and well-being. I have always admired the way you are comfortable speaking your mind, asking questions, and being so knowledgeable on the topics you really care about. You are a strong woman, Grams. I think I inherited that from you.

More time passed after Mother's birthday, and still there was only the same chatty, friendly, protected talk of Sarah. Five months later, Sarah made a visit to her grandparents. She hoped to have a time to really talk. They laughed, played games, went to the movies, baked together, exercised together. There seemed to be no natural, easy way for Sarah to bring up the parts of her life she hadn't shared.

One night, Sarah and her grandparents had been chatting in the living room. When Grams and Gramps were talking about getting ready for bed, Sarah just pushed herself and said, "Before we go to sleep, can we talk?" The three of them sat in the living room, and Sarah began by saying how hurt she had felt and how she longed to share her life with them. They all spoke honestly—not easily, but honestly. My mother apologized that her response those years before had been an angry outburst. They all said they felt closer to each other than they had in years.

Sarah worried that after that conversation her sexuality would again become a forbidden topic. The next morning, Sarah said, "You two had a short night."

Grams said, "We can sleep when we're old. I'm glad we talked."

They kept talking. They went off to church together. Later, when Sarah was leaving for the airport, Mother invited her to bring her girlfriend on another visit.

I am grateful that my mother lived to have this healing with her granddaughter. When I tried to express this gratitude once, I slipped and said, "I am grateful that my mother lived to have this healing with her daughter." And that's true, too.

⬧

I WANTED SO MUCH from my mother. I wanted her love and attention, but I resented it that her life was so centered on me. I thought she babied me. When I was a child, she quizzed me for my tests at school, listened to my speeches, shopped with me and for me. Throughout my life, she made purchases not for herself but always for me. When she traveled, she always brought home little gifts for me and clearly had spent her time thinking of me and shopping for me.

Julia Ward Howe founded Mother's Day in 1870 as a protest against war. Mother marched with me in Vietnam War protests and demonstrated with me in peace moratoriums. Mother stood by me even when I made choices she did not understand and would not have chosen for me. Even though she didn't understand, Mother came around to standing by her granddaughter, whose partner is a woman. I can imagine Mother, if she had been able, walking with her daughter and granddaughter in a Gay Pride parade. Mother read books, drew, played games, attended performances, wrote cards and letters, baked zillions of chocolate chip cookies, and praised and supported not just me but my children as well.

I love my mother, deeply care for her, and feel immense gratitude to her for giving me life and raising me. I respect her for the life she lived. I have also felt angry, resentful, and dis-approving of her, and at times I distanced myself from her. And surely she felt all of these feelings toward me, too.

I wanted so much from my mother. I wanted nurturing love, acceptance of who I am. I wanted a balance of interest and attention and enough separation and distance that we each could be ourselves. No one person could give me all I wanted, though. Have any of us received all the love we wanted and deserved? Have any of us given all the love we have to give?

On Mother's Day in the year of her diagnosis, I tried to imagine life without my mother. This woman who was such a large, strong presence in my life now looked small and frail. I suppose I could have thought, I'll be free; I'll have no one I feel obligated to try to please. Actually, I was thinking, who will send me cards and letters? Who will tell me they are proud of me? Who will cheer me on? Who will be so fierce-ly loyal to me? Who will remember me as a baby and as a young girl?

Now, when I think of the times my mother seemed to pry into my life, I know she wanted to talk about things that were real and important to me. Even her arguments were a way to be engaged with me on things that mattered.

When I saw an advertisement for Mother's Day cards, my heart sank. Wouldn't I love to have her baby me even now?

✦

As I work in my study at the convent, I keep a candle lit. Immediately after Mother died, Sarah began to keep in her home a candle that was constantly lit, placed next to a photo-graph of her grandmother. In the photograph her grandmother is not as Sarah ever knew her. This is her grandmother before

Sarah was born, before I was born. Her grandmother is rowing a boat; she is a young woman about the age Sarah is now.

Sarah says that when she comes in at night, she says, "Hello, Grams," and when she wakes each new day, she says, "Good morning, Grams." On the eighty-second anniversary of her grandmother's birth, Sarah says, "I'm thinking of you, Grams." Sarah says she will keep the candle lit for one year.

These months after Mother's death, I am aware of her absence, aware of her presence. Her presence stays close over my daughter's house, over my brother's house, over my house, over me.

I am separate from my mother and continuing to relate to her.

At the end of her life, Mother's world was a hospital bed in one room of an apartment in a retirement home. The bed was too narrow, the paraphernalia too much. I couldn't get in bed and hold her. I hold her now inside me.

My life began, as George Eliot wrote, "waking up and loving my mother's face." As Mother was dying, she looked at her family, our faces showing love. I have looked death in the face, and it is the face of my mother. Mother—I carry her now in me as she once carried me in her.

On what would have been her eighty-second birthday, I bake a birthday cake. Some years back, Mother had cut out photographs of each family member and made little stands for them so they could be stuck into cakes as decorations. Whether family members could be present for celebrations or not, she remembered them in this way. I place Mother's photograph decorations on her cake, and we remember her.

*The desert shall rejoice, and blossom as the rose.*

—ISAIAH 35:1

I GO AND SIT in the empty chapel of the convent, look at the stained glass images, and wonder if the Bible stories I was taught as a child have meaning for me now.

As a baby, my parents presented me for baptism at the First Plymouth Congregational Church in Lincoln, Nebraska. My mother's family had been Congregationalist for several generations. My father's family was Catholic. As a little boy, though, my father was afraid of the nuns in their habits, so he walked away and into the church next to his home, First Plymouth.

I grew up in the church, and one day I turned my back on it and walked away. So much seemed elitist and limiting, hypocritical, patriarchal, irrelevant. So much seemed contradictory and convoluted. So much seemed baffling, bizarre, and bloody. I didn't want anything to do with it. I said no to all that and closed the door behind me. I walked away from the church of my childhood.

I spent time with friends, playing intellectual and critiquing it all. I turned to novels and poetry for meaning. I attended demonstrations and rallies and sought out adventures. I traveled around the world and learned something of other cultures and religions. I believed the truth couldn't be contained in any one form.

But when I gave birth to a daughter and then a son, I joined a church to provide them with a spiritual community. I found there a home to support my learning and growth. With that community's encouragement, I entered theological school and became a minister. Growing up in the Congregational Church gave me roots in the Jewish and Christian heritage. My Unitarian Universalist faith has grown out of this heritage.

Last year I was feeling frustrated as I worked on a sermon. I wanted to turn to a source book and read what it had to say on the theme I was writing about. I wanted a starting point for my own reflection. The religious freedom I knew and loved provided me with all the source books in the world. I could turn to any or all of the world's great religions and the commentaries and studies about them—poetry, novels, essays, the newspaper, the research of scientists and sociologists, the lives of exemplary women and men—all the learning of human beings. I felt like grieving. Having all the source books felt like having none at all.

That night I dreamed my daughter was pregnant, laboring, bringing forth multiple births. There were six babies, all of them emaciated and weak, none likely to survive. One of the six babies had a little more weight and substance than the others. In the dream, my daughter and I had the responsibility for these babies. Should we try to nourish and nurture them all against the odds of any surviving, or should we strengthen the one that was likely to thrive?

In the dream, I was a grandmother. The cycle of life turns. My daughter becomes the mother, and I become the grandmother. In reality, my energy is different from when I was younger. The time of my life is limited. How can I nourish my interest in all the great religions and other great sources of learning and truth? Without denying the other truths, perhaps I have to strengthen the truth that for me is already a little filled out—even if it is still an infant and needs lots of attention to develop.

In the last two decades, the writings of many individuals— Alice Walker, Matthew Fox, Martin Buber, Paul Tillich, Bob Kimball, and many others—gave me freer access to my Jewish and Christian roots. My dream urged me to tend and nurture those connections. My roots in the Jewish and

Christian tradition help sustain the growth of my religious identity. No cutting off at the roots, no blockage. A yes to my heritage allows a yes to my growth.

Many of us religious liberals who grew up in the Jewish and Christian tradition walked away from it. We threw it all out—the baby with the bathwater. I want to draw the baby out of the water and see what promise that baby holds.

❖

AFTER MOTHER DIED, I wanted to attend an Ash Wednesday service. Ash Wednesday marks the beginning of Lent, which commemorates Jesus' forty days in the desert, when he wrestled with the meaning of life and death and figured out who he was. Ash Wednesday reminds us that our lives are fleeting. Out of ashes we came, and to ashes we return.

I wanted a ritual to mark that I had been touched by death. I wanted to understand the meaning of my mother's living and dying in the Christian context of Lent and Easter. I wanted to understand how Mother could go from being such a strong, powerful woman to nothing at all—just dust and ashes.

My friend Lowell and I walked the Berkeley hills to All Souls Episcopal Parish for an Ash Wednesday service. We kneeled, and the priest made his way up and down the aisles, touching each forehead with ashes. He came to our row. He touched the foreheads of the people to my left and then worked his way behind us. He touched the foreheads of the people to my right and then worked his way in front of us. "Ashes to ashes, dust to dust," he spoke. I leaned in his direction so he could reach me. He moved throughout the room, but he never marked my forehead with ashes. If this were a dream, I asked myself, what would this omission mean? What would it mean, this not being seen, this not being touched?

When Mother was dying, my brother imagined being seen by her and receiving a last blessing. He imagined that Mother would reach out and hold his face in her hands, touch his forehead, and say, "You are my beloved; on you my favor rests." My brother says that actually, her last words to him were, "You have bad breath."

I too wanted my mother's blessing. I wanted her to touch her hands to my head, give thanks, and bless me. I wanted her to call on her mother, and her mother's mother, and all of humanity's good women and men of prophetic and poetic voice and courageous deed to watch over me. I wanted her to invite the breeze moving through my hair to uplift me and the ground beneath my feet to support me. I wanted to come home and receive my blessing.

On that Ash Wednesday, we all rose from our bent knees to sing. Lowell turned toward me and saw my unmarked forehead. She touched her fingers to her forehead and then

to mine, and she looked me in the eyes. She said, "You're
beautiful," and she blessed me.

HERE AT THE CONVENT, I am either inside writing or outside
walking, and I am always thinking about my mother. On a
walk I find a delicate, heart-shaped pink stone.

I enjoy friendly talk with several of the sisters. I write my
father and tell him he didn't need to be afraid of them when
he was a boy. He responds, "What about the sisters you don't
talk to?"

I ask the sisters how old they were when they became sisters. Some of the old women respond that they were eleven
and twelve years old. I ask if people can join at any age, say,
sixty. Sister Angela says, "Don't go getting any ideas."

The sisters say they want to nourish me physically and
spiritually. They want me to leave here having gained some
weight. They say they equate giving good food and giving love.
They remind me of my mother. I say, "You know, you can get
spiritually and physically flabby." I say, "I was hoping to leave
here having lost some weight." Sister Raphael, who is eighty-
four years old, says, "Burn it off. Walk it off."

I walk the grounds of the convent and center. There is a
sign that says, "An Invitation to Walk with Jesus." The walk is up

the hillside and includes the stations of the cross. The stations of the cross were created initially for people who could not make a pilgrimage to the Holy Land. The fourteen stages of the cross are a kind of miniature pilgrimage. I have been in churches and centers with the stations of the cross, but I have avoided them. You know—too negative, too bloody.

I walk the stations of the cross at the convent. I walk along a gentle slope to the granite markers carved with the last scenes of Jesus' life. I walk up to the first station: "Jesus is condemned, bearing the burden of false accusations and misunderstanding." I wonder how my mother and I misunderstood each other? Can any human being ever be fully understood?

The next two stations are close together: "Jesus carries the cross and embraces the suffering of the world. Jesus falls the first time and experiences the overwhelming effects of frailty and weakness." As I read, I picture my mother in her frailty and weakness. I remember her falls. Her suffering connected our family with the suffering of the world.

A bench faces the next stone, inviting a rest. I read, "Jesus meets his mother. Profound love heightens the intense sorrow felt in the face of another's suffering."

As I walk on to the fifth station, a hawk circles the blue sky over my head: "Simon helps Jesus carry his cross. Sharing life's burdens provides the opportunity of loving, self-giving, and oneness with Christ."

The path leads gently around the convent and retreat center to station six: "Veronica wipes the face of Jesus. Love empowers one to self-giving and courageous service."

As I climb the hillside on the way to the next station in the distance, I spot two coyotes running through the dried-up vineyards. "Jesus falls the second time. Jesus knows the pain of human struggle and suffering." Then, "Jesus meets the women. Grief and sorrow at the affliction of a loved one call for tenderness and affection." Tears come to my eyes as I remember Sarah and Ben gently, patiently, tenderly caring for their Grams.

I read the ninth marker: "Jesus falls the third time. The plight of a despairing humanity cries for a loving and compassionate response." Mother's dying took us into the hospital, the nursing home, and the retirement home to see some of the world's suffering and the need for compassion.

I walk on: "Jesus is stripped. Stripped of illusions, one comes to discover ultimate freedom in God." Mother let go of everything—her possessions, her body, her mind.

Jesus' death is marked on the eleventh and twelfth stones: "Jesus is nailed to the cross, outstretched in open and loved-filled embrace. Jesus offers humanity its salvation.

"Jesus dies on the cross and lives out for us the paradox of death events turned into life-filled sources." How have the events of my mother's death turned into life-filled sources?

I look out over the distance and see a tumbleweed gently rolling along: "Jesus is taken from the cross. To engage in the liberation of human suffering will challenge the quality of your life."

The fourteenth station of the cross is this: "Jesus is buried. Rest your burdens in deep inner peace and wait for the fulfillment of God's plan." Here in the desert, among the sisters, in my study, on my walks, and in my narrow little bed, I rest my burden.

On the top of the highest hill on the immediate grounds of the center is a final station.

The text reads, "Jesus rises from the dead. Ultimate freedom and joy are found in the way, the truth, and the life."

Just beyond this final station is an opening in the fence. I duck under the wire and wander the vineyards and the neighboring hills. I walk up and down the hillsides, thinking of my mother. I feel her suffering and death, and I open my heart to the suffering and death of Jesus. I imagine my walk, my pilgrimage, not as the stations of the cross but as the openings of the heart.

BEYOND THE FINAL STATION of the cross, beyond the boundaries of the convent and retreat, I go out under the wire in an opening in the fence to wander the hills and vineyards. I wander through my memories of my mother's living and dying.

I imagine someone sees me and asks me if I'm lost, or what I'm doing, or what I'm looking for. I imagine I answer that "I am looking for a message from my mother." I'm keeping my ears awake to whatever I hear. I'm keeping my eyes open to all I see.

On these hills I look into the soft eyes of goats. I see a roadrunner, an owl, the whirl of an iridescent green and blue hummingbird. I see and hear the rush of fluttering wings of quail and a swarm of blackbirds above my head, encircling me—all those wings stirring and flapping at once. I see a glorious V of flying cranes crossing the sky, a tree full of shiny, smooth, dark green avocados; the sunset glow on the distant mountains, a lone green stalk in acres of sand and dust with a tall purple blossom; a rock standing out among all the others, brilliant in the morning sunlight.

I pick up objects as I walk and give them meaning. One day, on a road, I pick up a golf ball. Mother was a golfer. When I played golf with her as a child she could always spot my lost balls. The next day I spot another golf ball in a ditch and then a third, miles away in a row of vineyards. I imagine I will have completed this journey, like the fourteen stages of the cross, when I have found fourteen golf balls. Or maybe it should be eighteen. You know—the stations of the course.

I am walking and writing, finding meaning in the objects I come across, making this retreat my pilgrimage.

◈

WHEN MOTHER WAS DYING, Holy Week on the Christian calendar became my own holy week. On the roller-coaster ride on which cancer and strokes took my mother, Palm Sunday was a down day, and she didn't have the energy to get out of her nightgown and off the couch. Charlie, Sarah, and I were worshipping at the Congregational Church of my childhood in Lincoln, Nebraska. The Plymouth Brass played, the children's choir waved palm branches as they sang, and the minister preached on the difference between heroes and celebrities. My father got teary, and so did I, as we acknowledged that this was the first time he had come to church without my mother.

During the hymn after the sermon, the color drained out of my father's face. He took out his nitroglycerin and swallowed a small pill. The congregation sat down, but Dad and I remained standing. His hands were rigid and tight on the pew in front of him. Then he started to topple over toward me. I started to cry, but Sarah stayed calm and strong. A wheelchair was offered, 911 was called, and Dad was rolled down the aisle as the service continued. Charlie had had a history of heart problems, but this time his heart checked out okay.

"The fast one he pulled at church," as my mother later called it, was not a heart attack but a heartbreak.

This was the week that Sarah and I were in Nebraska to help my parents move to the retirement home. We had been helping my parents sort through a lifetime accumulation of photographs, letters, and cards. My parents were being so noble in taking care of everything as they sorted through and let go of their possessions—their lives as they had known them. They were being the kind of heroes about whom the minister preached.

That night Sarah and I massaged my mother's body. When we told my brother, who had cooked them consecrated homemade chicken soup on his visit the week before, he said, "Massage—now *that's* a sacrament." I got in bed and cried. Tears—now, *that's* holy water.

WHEN SARAH AND I returned from that visit later in the week, I went straight to church. I called my parents. No matter how old we all are, our parents are still our parents, and they want to know their children and grandchildren got home safely.

In that phone call I learned that in the late afternoon, my parents had been sitting outside in the sunshine, and Mother's right leg gave out when they were about to come into the house. My father had managed to help her up the stairs to bed. "I should be there now," I thought. "How could this have happened right after I left?"

The day was *Maundy Thursday* on the Christian calendar. As a child, I thought people were saying Monday Thursday. Maundy Thursday commemorates the anniversary of the Passover supper that Jesus ate as his last supper. *Maundy* comes from the Latin for "mandate"—mandating, or establishing, the institution of the Eucharist as the gathered community sharing the meal. Jesus washed the feet of his disciples, and in some churches Maundy Thursday involves the washing of one another's feet. To let someone wash your feet is to be vulnerable and open to intimate touch. Weary, aching feet receive tender care and are held, cleansed, caressed, and soothed. On our visit home, my daughter and I had rubbed Mother's feet with fragrant lotions.

I went directly from the airport to church that day because in our congregation, every Thursday evening people gather. Dinner is served, followed by a worship service and programs. During this community meal, people came up and gave me hugs. Their touch was comforting, and the laying on of their hands was healing. People spoke kind, caring words. With each tender contact, I started weeping. I cried because my mother was dying and because I knew these good people. They had also opened their lives to me. I knew their losses and sorrows, their hopes and dreams. How else do you make a church community but through the sharing of meals and lives?

✦

THE DAY FOLLOWING Maundy Thursday is Good Friday. When I called my folks that morning, no one answered the phone.

I knew Mother had had difficulty the day before in getting up out of a chair. I called the hospital. The only times my mother had ever been hospitalized in her life were for the births of her babies. When we were young children, she spent every day for two years at the hospital caring for my father. In their retirement, they have spent years volunteering at the hospital. Now Mother was a patient. That morning my father had tried to help Mother to the bathroom, and they couldn't manage. In response to a 911 call, four men carried Mother out of the house. She had had another stroke and was in the hospital with her right arm and leg paralyzed. This felt like the beginning of the end.

The word *Good* for this Friday is unsettling. In some traditions and languages it is called Sorrow Friday or Long Friday, because it marks Jesus' long passage into death. People gather in dark sanctuaries, hear lamentations, and watch candles slowly go out, one by one.

✦

WHAT HAPPENS WHEN PEOPLE DIE? What will happen when I die? On Easter Sunday morning, the stone was rolled away, and the tomb was empty.

The first time I heard the gospel song "Roll Away the Rock," I wasn't at a church. I was at an early morning exercise class. I thought the words of the song were "Throw away the rocks," and I loved it! I pictured myself throwing away the knotty rocks of tension in my neck and shoulders. I was moving wildly and freely, feeling fully alive.

I don't know what happens when we die. I do know when I am most alive. I know moments of feeling connected with all that is. I feel out of myself and most wholly myself. Time, as I know it, has ended, and I glimpse time out of time; I taste eternity. Perhaps in those moments I experience what is true always. I am, you are, one with the holy, with the mystery, with creation and creativity. How could God not always be among us? What I want is to try for more and more moments. I want to take a moment to touch someone I love. Hold someone's face in my hands. Look someone in the eyes. Kiss a forehead. Offer a blessing. As the gospel song says, "Bring my heart out of prison, let me praise again. Fill my empty soul with love. I want to see the light, tell the truth, walk the path, roll away the rock from my soul." And whatever happens, all will be all right.

During Mother's funeral, when Glen Miller's *Stardust* was playing, Sarah saw her grandmother, my mother, restored in health and vitality, dancing above her casket—dancing more freely than she had ever danced before.

⬥

WHEN I RETURNED HOME after Mother's memorial service, I played the tape Bruce had made of music Mother loved. "Unforgettable," the duet by Nat King Cole and his daughter Natalie, was made after he had died, using his original recording. I select a cloth, lay down on the floor, and hold the cloth as if I am able to get into Mother's hospital bed in her room in the retirement home and hold her. The tape of music plays on, I begin to dance with Mother, and then I become Mother dancing. I am Mother dancing with Ben, with Sarah, with Charlie, and with Bill. I am Mother dancing with me, reaching out, clasping hands, holding on and letting go. Her hands are holding my face, blessing the soft, wild aura of long, wiry gray hair around my head. In the dance, my body is her body. She moves in me like blood through my veins, like wine pouring into the cup, like bread rising in the warm kitchen. I am Mother dancing. I am Mother dancing with my brother, his son, her grandson. I am Mother reaching out to take the hands of her great-granddaughter. In my dancing we are all encircling her, and she is dancing around, being caught and upheld by all of us.

She is dancing freely, playfully, fully, blessing and being blessed.

IN THE LAST MONTHS of Mother's life, one of the pleasures she had was being bathed. She was carried out of her wheelchair; held in the arms of a large, strong woman; lifted up; and then immersed in a hot whirlpool bath. The retirement home had rules about how many minutes long the bath could be, and the woman had other patients to serve, but Mother did not want to be carried out of the pool. She soaked up every minute with pleasurable oohs and aahs.

At the water ceremony at our church at the end of each summer, we give thanks for being part of the stream of life. We give thanks for green pastures and still waters that restore our souls. We give thanks for community where together we can share tears of joy and tears of sorrow. We pray to work for justice to roll down like waters and for peace like an everflowing stream. I say that water in all its forms is healing—as ocean, as rain, as sweat, as tears. I like to quote Nebraska naturalist Loren Eiseley: "If there is magic on this planet, it is contained in water." Birth waters hold us before we enter the world. Water holds the earth we call home, our final resting place.

In the last hours of Mother's life, Sarah and I bathed her. I washed her hair, and we anointed her body with lotion. We sang her to sleep. We sang the Cris Williamson lullaby that I sang to Sarah when she was a child: "We'll rock on the water, I'll cradle you deep, and hold you while angels sing you to sleep."

A month after Mother's death, I dreamed I was holding her; cradling her frail, birdlike body; carrying her into a pool; walking and bearing her through healing waters. In the dream, I reached out to my mother, and she trusted her body to me. I felt the strength of my arms as I held her. She was totally accepting of this dependence on me. I felt her let go and release herself to me. There is nothing quite like this holding, this walking—healing and being healed—this immersion in holy water.

AS THE STORY GOES, fifty days after Jesus' death, the followers were all in one place. A great wind came and filled the entire house where they were. They were filled with the Spirit of Life. Each began speaking in different tongues, but unlike the story of the Tower of Babel, in which there was no understanding but only racket, Jesus' followers could understand one another. The story of the coming of the Spirit is celebrated in the Christian liturgical calendar as Pentecost, and it holds forth the promise that we all can understand one another.

I can't remember my mother changing my diaper or nursing me. I can remember her changing my bedding after I got sick in bed in the night, bathing me, rocking me, and saying prayers with me. I witnessed her changing my children's diapers, rocking them, holding them, playing with them, reading to them, loving them, and laughing with them, and I know she did all this for me, too.

Mother fought fiercely for what she thought was right. Yet she was capable of forgiveness and reconciliation.

Mother was blessed to have lived long enough to have had role reversals with her husband. After years of caring for him, she received his care in the end. After years of her being talkative, he became the one to talk on the phone to friends and family. She was blessed to receive from her children and grandchildren, for there finally to be some mutuality, some reciprocity. We cooked, cleaned, and even sewed for her. Her standards eased, and she was grateful for help. We bathed her, changed her diapers, rinsed out her clothes, and got her to do her exercises, use her walker, and then use her wheelchair.

Mother was strong. In a lifetime of vitality and hard work and in the last months of frailty and weakness, Mother was strong. Shortly after the birth of her first child, her husband was drafted and served in World War II, away from home for two and a half years. Not many years after his return, she experienced the death of her favorite and younger brother, followed by the death of the father she dearly loved. At the same time, her husband was hospitalized for two years. She had two young children; she was nursing her husband, making decisions, keeping house, raising kids, working. What courage!

Mother didn't sit still. She was always wiping the counter, picking up, cleaning up.

What love!

I dream I have destroyed someone and I am sitting in the basement, in the ruins of what I have done, knowing that I, too, am capable of doing the worst that human beings are capable of doing. The dream is terrifying; this power to destroy is awful. Yet in the dream I also know that I am capable of doing the best that human beings are capable of doing. The dream is illuminating; this power to create is awe-full. I find both monsters and gods in myself. What I saw in my mother, I see in me.

I want the Spirit of Life to come to me, as in the much-loved Carolyn McDade hymn: "Spirit of Life, Come unto me, sing in my heart all the stirrings of compassion." Like the followers of Jesus understanding each other through their differences, fifty days after Mother's death, I grow in under-standing her.

◈

THE SEASONS CIRCLE AROUND. This year on the Sunday after Ash Wednesday, I preached on what I was giving up. I vowed to use the forty days of Lent to give up some of the excess of the previous months, to turn toward an ordered life. I had recently dreamed I was trying to pull on a girdle and was spilling out of it; then I was trying to find a way to pull on a second girdle in the other direction. I was feeling both physi-cally and spiritually flabby.

Since my mother died, I had ridden waves of emotions. Sometimes I would think, "You've lost your mother. You deserve some comfort. Mother was always good at showing love and comfort by offering baked goods, so have a piece of cake or some cookies—or why go through all that in-between time of preparing and baking; just rip open the bag of chocolate chips."

I believe in letting oneself have a little time—time to be angry, time to cry, time to heal, even time to be a little self-indulgent and lazy. And I'm pretty good at extending that time. At New Year's, I thought, "I'm just not ready yet." Now with Lent, I thought I was ready to get back into a structured, self-disciplined practice to begin each day, to secure my life and set it right. I wrote out my grocery list: "fruits and vegeta-bles, no cheese, no ice cream." Then I realized that Ash Wednesday was still a week away, and I went into the kitchen and ate a handful of chocolate chips.

Lent began. No longer would I use the stresses and busy-ness of the days, the rain, old hurts and losses, or Mother as an excuse. My Lenten sermon was well received. As people were coming out of the sanctuary, a number of them spoke of how the sermon touched their own needs for discipline and order. I was feeling pretty good.

One woman asked to speak to me right away. We went into my office, and she began weeping and wondering if she was ever going to get it right. "Will I always be trying and falling short?" she asked between deep sobs. Then she looked up and said, "Is your dress on backwards?" And it was! Her tears let up. We both laughed.

I'm never going to get it totally right. Nobody ever is. We are always going to be trying. Just when I think I'm there, there will be one more thing to let go of. There will be some self-important image of myself to give up. There will be new losses to grieve, new life to meet. I know I'll make mistakes. I'll overeat again; I'll skip my morning practice. Much as I want to believe it won't happen, I might even show up a second time at church with my dress on backwards. Forty days after Ash Wednesday, a structured, self-disciplined practice seems not so much to secure my life as to prepare the way for whatever comes.

◈

I KEEP LEARNING from my parents. After Mother's death, my father moved to a smaller apartment in the retirement home. He has been learning to live without the physical presence of his wife of nearly sixty years. Now, seven months after her death, my father is letting go of even the last of his familiar furniture, letting go of the community where he has lived almost all of his eighty-one years. He is letting go of all that has been; he is moving across the country to a retirement home in California, near us.

On Saturday mornings when I was a little girl, I would walk with my father into the old classic, marble-pillared downtown post office. He knew everyone. I felt like I was at City Hall with the mayor of Lincoln, Nebraska. Now my father is letting go of this place where he has been known and loved.

My father has worked nearly all his life, managing grocery stores and then owning hardware stores. After retiring, he worked at another hardware store, and for fifteen years he has volunteered regularly at a hospital. He is letting go of roots and identity. He is letting go of his Congregational church. He is letting go of the wide open prairie where

Mother is buried. He is letting go of the streets and sites that he knows like the back of his hand.

The leaving is full of little deaths. As hard as it must be to let go of all those things, my father knows those things were the life that was. He is letting go, moving toward what is not so known and secure—what is more mysterious, open. He is teaching me that if you are alive and choose life, there is more change ahead. Life doesn't hold still and proclaim, "Now you've made it; you're here." Life demands not acquiring but letting go.

"WANT, WANT, WANT. All you do is want," I hear a mother at a grocery store complain to her child. All you do is want.

As a theology student, I was asked to state my credo on the traditional theological categories of the Divine, the Human, the Christ, the Church, and the End. Through the course of the semester, taking in the readings, the words of the professor, and the thoughts of my classmates, I came to state my credo simply:

The Divine:   I want.
The Human:  I find limits (in myself, in others).
The Christ:    What I want is possible.
The Church:  What I want for myself, I want for others.

I wasn't sure what to say about the End. My own experience of endings was that they were only beginnings. I am now coming to trust:

The End:   What I want has been there from
           the beginning.

Wanting and desiring are good. Wanting is what it means to be alive. We want to be awake and aware; we want to see and be seen, to love and be loved. Wanting leads us to the Divine. The nature of being human is to slam up against limits. We feel unloved and unloving. We aren't being seen for who we truly are. We feel only half awake. Still, there is an irrepressible spirit that stirs in us, leading us to trust that what we want is possible. In relationships, in community, we begin to want for others what we want for ourselves. And the meaning of *others* expands to include more and more. Love knows no boundaries. We have moments—glimpses—of knowing that what we want is true. Every bush is holy; every life is sacred; everyone is loved. The moments can steadily grow, and we can come home to this knowing.

I call out my own version of the Twenty-third Psalm:

Love is my companion.
I shall not want.
Love rests with me in green pastures

and walks with me beside still waters.
Love restores my soul.
Love leads me in paths of justice for its name's sake.
Even though I walk through the valley of the shadow
     of death,
I fear not for Love is with me.
Love's arms reach out for me and comfort me.
Even in the desert, Love prepares a table before me.
Love anoints my head with oil.
My cup overflows.
Surely goodness and mercy will follow me all the days
     of my life
and I will dwell in the house of Love forever.

AFTER FORTY YEARS, I finally got a summer hairdo. The wild and woolly mane was shorn.

The young woman who cut my hair asked me to take a deep breath, because, she said, hair is very connected to our identities. Then she took the whole long, wiry gray mass in one hand and, with the other, cut it off.

In the mirror, I could see both myself at ten and my mother at eighty. Ten was the last time I had my hair short. In the mirror, I could still catch a glimpse of that same bewildered, lost kid I sometimes was. In the mirror, I could see the old woman I was becoming.

All the gray short-haired old women (like me) love my haircut: "Oh, Barbara, I love your hair!" One said, "Ever since I met you I have been wanting you to get your hair cut." But people will say just about anything to me: "You look like the back end of a plucked chicken!" "What did you do? Back into a fan?" "I know you're perimenopausal, because you got your hair cut." "Does this mean the revolution is over?" "Somebody has been seeing a lesbian hair stylist." "As a child of the sixties, I don't like this." "What does *Bill* think of this?" "Oh no, oh no, oh no! Why on earth did you do such a thing?"

Why *did* I do such a thing? The truth is, it was impulse. Sarah, who was preparing for a first and solo trip to Europe, asked me to accompany her for moral support as she got her hair cut. When we met at the shop, she said she couldn't do it. I told her she didn't need to. Her hair would be no problem in traveling. I told her I would take the appointment and get my hair cut.

The truth is, it was a long, slow decision. For years I had been saying that maybe I should just get the whole thing cut short.

This haircut was a mother-daughter event. There was the flesh-and-blood presence of Sarah and the mind-and-heart presence of my mother, who had died nine months before. Of course, Mother would turn up for my big haircut.

During my late childhood and early teen years, Mother escorted me to get my hair professionally straightened. We also ironed my hair, fried it with electric curlers, rolled it around orange juice cans, coated it with mayonnaise, tied weights on it, stretched a panty hose over it at night to hold it down, glued it down with gels, did everything we could to tame and control it. This was hair wilder than Jesus wore it. My hair was sleek and smooth until I got excited, ran freely, danced with abandon, or rode in a convertible. The kinks and curls, waves and frizz then came back to life. Finally, I made peace with my hair and just let it go wild.

Mother didn't talk much in the last months of her life. Still, when I arrived on one of my last visits, she managed to say, "I'm not going to tell you for the millionth time: Get your hair cut."

The young woman who cut my hair talked as she clipped. She had had quite a year: Her house and possessions were lost in a fire, she and her partner (she *is* a lesbian hair stylist) broke up, and her mother died. While hearing about her year, my hair didn't seem like much to let go of.

So why didn't I get my hair cut while my mother was still alive? After all those years of fighting my hair, I was sick of people trying to control it. Even strangers would walk up to me and say, "Did you know you can get hair professionally straightened?" I just wanted to let my hair be. Some sort of power resided in my hair, and I didn't want it stolen away like

Samson's hair and strength were by Delilah. And I was defiant with my hair, like daughters are with mothers.

In the last years, I witnessed my mother gradually let go of everything. If I could let go of a trademark—of something closely identified with myself—perhaps I would do okay with all there was ahead for me to let go of.

In biblical times, a common rite of mourning was tonsuring, clipping the hair or shaving the head, to grieve like a child. Few people alive have any memory of me as a baby. I am a motherless child. I cut my hair as a rite of mourning. Cutting my hair marked the end of one time of my life and entry into another time. This haircut, "the gray helmet," crowned me as the oldest living female in our family.

Even with change, much remains the same. When people ask me how I like my haircut, I say it is still my hair. There have always been qualities I like about my hair and qualities I don't like. That's still true. But in the mirror, I see eternity. I am ten and fifty and eighty. And Mother, gone since fall, looks back at me.

THE SUMMER AFTER Mother's death, I led a summer pilgrimage to our partner church in Transylvania, a region in Romania.

On the pilgrimage I was called tour leader, but I felt like an impostor. So much of the tour was out of my control; so much was out of my range of knowledge. Who was I to teach Transylvanian Unitarian history? As a courtesy, I had been invited to preach in the big city of Kolozsvar. Who was I to preach at the cathedral church of Unitarians in Transylvania? Tour leader, historian, preacher to people whose lives I did not know—those roles were not my natural fiber! I felt like a child caught in a nightmare.

The night before I was to preach, I dreamed I was wearing only a little black slip. I was in a school, in a classroom full of lively students, as the substitute teacher. I was trying to act like I knew what I was doing, but I didn't even know what class it was, and I was trying to find out. A student told me the class was "Meter and Syntax." "Meter and syntax . . . meter and syntax," I kept thinking. "Whoa, like iambic pentameter. How am I going to fake my way through this?" The scene changed, and some people were draping a big cape around me. The cape was made of some fabric like burlap or linen or muslin—some sort of natural fiber. People stood back as I walked forward. And someone said, "Now, you're the pope!" I was thinking, "Oh, my God! No way can I fake this."

Sunday morning arrived. I woke with diarrhea, not from the foreign foods and water but from my uneasiness. My mind was racing, and I was making last-minute changes to the sermon. It had been sent in advance to be translated. Transylvanian Eva Keleman, the real tour leader, graciously translated my last-minute changes. The Reverend Ferenc Balint-Benczedi, the minister of the church, was warm and kind. The plan was that he would read a translation of my words after each paragraph. When I showed him the last-minute changes, he put me at ease by saying how alike we were. He said he always woke up on Sunday knowing the changes he must make to the sermon.

Ferenc placed around my shoulders one of those heavy, black, Transylvanian clergy capes. It looked to me like something belonging to the religious sect in *Babette's Feast* or to the clergy in *The Scarlet Letter*—serious, weighty, and foreboding.

I teetered my way up the spiral stairs into the high stone pulpit. I was praying I wouldn't trip on the cape, that I wouldn't have to flee for the bathroom, and that something larger than me would speak through my lips and hear through the congregation's ears. I prayed to be persuaded by my own sermon's message that we all are one body and love prevails.

The faces of the congregation—Transylvanian Unitarians and members of the tour group—held and supported me. After the service, an old Transylvanian man, with tears in his eyes, said in English, "I love you, too."

WE LEFT KOLOZSVAR and traveled to Homorodujfalu, the small village of our partner church. The first night in the village, I dreamed I was shopping with my mother and grandmother. We were shopping in an old downtown department store where my mother and I had often shopped for me. After my grandfather died, my grandmother moved from her little town to the city and got a job as the doll salesperson in the store's toy department.

In the dream, my mother and grandmother were at their best: at ease, good-humored, good-spirited. Other shoppers and a clerk were equally at ease and comfortable with one another. The clerk invited me to try on a long sweater coat that she said was perfect on my grandmother and my mother. She thought it would be just right for me, too, but I thought, "If it fit them, it won't fit me." I saw that the sweater coat was tan with orange and red designs along the border—not a color or style I would normally wear. But when I put on the coat, it fit and was beautiful. It was just right, a natural. I knew it would be of use to me and that I would like wearing it.

I woke up, remembering the dream first as a mundane shopping dream. But as I remembered the details, tears came to my eyes. The presence of my grandmother and mother had felt so real, so natural. I no longer felt like an impostor in a cape that was not my natural fiber. I was ready to take up the cloak of my mother and her mother.

On this second Sunday of the pilgrimage, we were going to church in the village. I had been invited to offer a prayer. On Friday I had written a short prayer and asked our translator, Laslo, to write it in Hungarian. He tutored me in the pronunciation. Our host, Judit, and her mother, Luisa, coached me. All the village women helped me though they were hard at work in the kitchen preparing food for the next day's celebration. When it came to Hungarian, I was not a natural. I grew confident, though, that if I stumbled during the service, all these women who had learned the prayer by heart would call out the words. My playful, loving relationship with Laslo, with Judit and Luisa, and with the women of the village was a good fit, a natural.

On Sunday morning, Luisa placed around my shoulders a natural-fiber, gray and tan woven stole embroidered by the village women with red flowers, hearts, and a chalice. Luisa lovingly straightened it; smiled and gave me a nod of confidence.

After the service, a colleague also in attendance told me that my pronunciation sounded like Hebrew. Another patted my hand, saying I was very brave. Eva, our tour leader, told me she had to guess at some of the words. Still, I want to believe that just being willing to be taught and being willing to try gave a message: "O God, in the light of these people's eyes, you shine. In hospitality, you reside. In the meeting of people of different languages, you rejoice. In hard work, you act. Wherever love is, you are." During the service I was held by a circle of women. A mother and her daughter and a host of women cloaked me with their tender care.

❖

THAT SUMMER AFTER my mother died I took a seminary course taught by theologian Marcus Borg. Borg talks of the pre-Easter and the post-Easter Jesus. The pre-Easter Jesus is the remarkable historical person who is now dead and gone. Borg holds up this historical figure and celebrates the humanity of Jesus, both for his greatness and ours. Borg believes there is nothing Jesus did that some other human being couldn't possibly do.

The post-Easter Jesus is what Jesus became after his death—the mythological, metaphorical Jesus. The post-Easter Jesus is spoken of with the language of lovers. When you are in love, you might say, "My guy is the most beautiful person in the world." And others might respond, "Huh?" This is the language John Hick calls "the poetry of devotion and the hyperbole of the heart." Jesus was the light of the world. He was the son of God.

Metaphors are fingers pointing to the moon. The metaphors surrounding Jesus were created first by people closest to him so they could speak of their experience of his life and death. How can I understand the metaphors? To what truths do they point?

It has been almost one year since my mother died. Reflecting on Mother's death helps me understand the ways the people closest to Jesus talked about him. I experience my mother's love as a reflection of a larger love that does not and cannot die. We, the people closest to her, experienced Mother's suffering, her detachment, her surrender, and her death, and we experience her continued presence.

Her death has meaning for us, her family, and in a certain way her death was "good" for us. Her death brought the family together and brought out people's strengths. Her death encouraged us to see that life is short and to see the importance of tending to what really matters. And so, in a certain way, Mother died so we might live. Her death was a life-bringing event. Losing her, I am also finding her with my perspective widened, softened, set free. Losing her, I am finding myself.

In a certain way she died for us. I believe that my death— that each of our deaths—will also bring meaning to others. We will die for others.

Mother's death leads me to believe there is something more than death. Love continues.

In the celebration of the bread and the wine, Jesus' followers remember him. Similarly, when our family sits down to a meal, we remember Mother and all the feasts she laid before us.

My daughter said that at Mother's funeral, as 1940s big band dance music played, she saw her grandmother restored to health, more alive than she had ever been, dancing above her casket. I have never asked my daughter what she means when she says that she saw her grandmother. After experiencing my mother as weak and frail and dying, I am glad my daughter can remember her as strong and whole and alive.

So this must be what Jesus' followers meant when they spoke of their love of him and his impact on their lives. Our family's experience with death opens a doorway for me to understand the truths beneath the metaphors, the signs that point the way.

JESUS TAUGHT US LOVE of God, neighbor, and self. The Easter story, the story of Jesus told as love embodied, might go like this:

> Love is among people, attracting a following. Love moves beyond the usual boundaries, healing the hurting, feeding the hungry, teaching people to live more fully. You know love can heal. You feel one with the person in front of you, one with the beauty around

you, one with all that is. Love makes you feel more alive. Love leads you to trust. When you feel loved and loving, there is no resentment, no reaching out to hurt or harm. You see love's promise.

In the story, when love comes to town, love is welcomed and praised. But almost before you can say "Hail and hosanna," love is betrayed, denied, ridiculed, condemned, and crucified. Love can be just that scary. Love means change, and it disrupts the status quo.

Love dies. Loss, grief, and despair take over. Hearts and spirits are broken. Love is sealed up in a tomb—and then love disappears. What remains is emptiness. You know about love disappearing and the emptiness that follows. Sometimes you try to fill the emptiness with hard work or with food and drink and pleasures and goods that never quite satisfy. Sometimes you withdraw even further. You are sealed off from the miracle of every day.

In the Easter story, after the disappearance, love's presence miraculously returns. Those whose faith had been shattered somehow, in community, pick up the broken pieces and carry on. Resurrection is this coming out of emptiness into relationship. The realm of love resides in you. Divine love is in your eyes and ears and fingertips. And it is not in you alone. Together we join our strengths to bring the realm of love to earth. When you want for others what you want for yourself, life and love return. You glimpse eternity.

The Easter story proclaims that love is the way. Whether it be two thousand years ago or today, whether it be between friends, between mother and child, or in community, love is the way. No one comes into the presence of what e. e. cummings calls "everything which is natural, which is infinite, which is yes" except by love.

I HAVE WALKED the desert all around the convent. At sunrise, at noon, at sunset, under the stars, under the waxing moon, in wind, and in mist, I have walked the hillsides, roads, vineyards, and neighboring ranches. I have gathered objects for an altar on my table. The finding of objects and the placing of them on an altar has been a playful, meaningful ritual. What fun I have had!

Early on I found a long, narrow, soft gray fabric that became the altar cloth. I was surprised to find a golf ball, but I picked it up, since my mother was a golfer. I was surprised to keep finding golf balls in ditches, on hilltops, in loose sand by the roadside, in brambles, and in the dusty rows between vineyards—in places miles apart. Someone must be turning these hills into a wide-open driving range.

On one walk, I found another of many golf balls. Finding them was getting almost boring, and without really looking at it, I placed the ball in my pocket. Ahead of me I could see twigs woven together as if someone had created the kind of crown of thorns you see in paintings of Jesus. When I reached it and turned it over, the twigs went from big ones to twigs that were smaller and smaller and softer and softer. I had found a deserted bird's nest. When I got back to the room, I slipped the golf ball into the nest and saw that someone had marked the ball with a big black question mark.

The altar has a puzzle piece, two golf balls, and the nest with the ball with the question mark. New life is full of possibility, full of uncertainty. Next to the nest is the husk of a gourd, the outer covering of a golf ball, and a cracked-open practice golf ball. From these hatched-open spheres a shiny, curly ribbon, runs across the length of the cloth like an umbilical chord.

Nearby is a card with a picture of Mary and Jesus—mother and child. Above the mother and child are golden orbs. The mother is dressed in a blue and red robe. The child holds a cluster of grapes. A star shines between their two heads. The crescent moon and a cloud are at the mother's feet. I have placed next to the picture two golden, round gourds that look like they are crowns of light, as well as a dried thistle for the star. Off to the side of the card are a blue stone, a piece of red clay, and a cluster of grapes.

Next are blooming desert wildflowers; a band of rainbow ribbon; a delicate, pink, heart-shaped stone; a soft gray feather; a snail's shell; a rock; and a cluster of golf balls, gathered like family or community. They are followed by a twig with many open pods, the seeds dispersed, as well as a scepter—a cruciform, magic wand–like branch with two pinecones still connected to the top. Each of these objects has reminded me of stories of my mother. I pick up two. Mother was strong like a rock and her presence now seems light like this feather.

The poet Robinson Jeffers writes of death as a letting go of what made one contract with pain and expand with pleasure: "That's gone, it is true; but all the rest is heightened, widened, set free." Mother is set free and like a bird wandering the air, leaving to the earth a feather. Each found object seems a love token to me from her.

MOTHER'S LAST WORDS to me each morning when I was a child leaving for school were, "Do you have a clean hanky? Do you have your lunch money?" As I got older, they were, "Don't stay out too late," "Be good," and always, "Drive carefully." I picture Mother waving goodbye at the front door, at the airport, on the driveway, at the train station. Her waves are a lament, a blessing, and a benediction.

She waved me off to the Peace Corps and to theological school. Her children and grandchildren moved far away, coming and going by train for annual summer visits. I had thought that Mother was grasping the reins, holding on too tight, not letting go of her children. I see now all the ways she was always saying goodbye, giving up control, letting go.

As Mother was dying, I made more visits. The miles between us were hard, and goodbyes became poignant. At the end of my summer visit, it was hard to part, but Mother sat up tall in her wheelchair and said, "Goodbye, Barb." She was direct, clear, and dry-eyed, with no last bits of advice, no strings attached. She was just acknowledging, releasing, saying goodbye. My father and I held each other with our eyes for a long time, tears flowing down our cheeks. A few months later, when I arrived at Mother's side, her hospice worker said, "She has been waiting for you to arrive so she can say goodbye."

Now, after her death, I feel her putting her hands lightly on top of my head and blessing me. She thanks God for me and for making her my mother. She knows my struggles and sees my mistakes in the larger picture of who I am, and there is nothing to forgive. I have always been free to be myself. She gives me her blessing and watches over me, along with my grandmother Ella Sophia, my great-grandmother Johanna, and my great-great-grandmother Little Oma. I will live in their love always.

WHAT IS MY INHERITANCE?

Ben and I visited my parents when they were still in their home, just beginning to go through things, knowing they were going to need to move. One evening after dinner, Mother brought to the table a drawer of jewelry. She began going through the jewelry, showing Ben and me each item. Here was her watch, given to her by her parents at her high school graduation. She graduated valedictorian in a class of thirty-nine students. The watch was broken. Here was the watch that was her mother's. It, too, was broken. Then a pocket watch that was her father's. Broken. There were other bits and pieces of costume jewelry. We all started laughing.

Ben reminded me that I buy cheap watches for a few dollars, wear them until the battery dies or the strap breaks, put them in a drawer, (because they could be fixed or the batteries could be replaced) and buy a new watch. We kept laughing— my inheritance.

My father told us a story I hadn't heard for a long time. Mother saved money for years and on their twenty-fifth anniversary, she gave him a ring with a diamond setting. As they approached their fortieth anniversary, my father wanted to give her a diamond ring. He couldn't afford it. He took the ring he received from her to a jewelry store and had the jeweler replace his diamond with glass and place the diamond in a setting for a ring for Mother. Mother loved the ring.

One night after my parents had worked all day in the yard, Mother looked down at Charlie's ring and noticed the "diamond" was missing. She insisted they go out and look through all the leaves, weeds, thorny branches, and clippings they had bagged. They spent hours looking for the diamond Charlie knew was glass. Charlie tried to persuade her to give up the search. She kept on for some time longer, combing each inch of their yard.

The ring was insured, and the next day Mother called the insurance agent to report the missing gem. When my father heard about the phone call, he told her the truth. She had the diamond returned to his ring. He wears it still.

My inheritance is rich in lasting love.

◈

BEFORE THIS TRIP to the desert, I wanted to have my forehead marked at an Ash Wednesday service. I wanted something visible to show I was marked by grief.

Staying here with the sisters, I dream that my friend Leslie approaches me. She stands out. She is wearing something like the dark blue habit of the sisters, but with a sackcloth tied with thorny vines around her waist. Her clothing is torn, and she has ashes smeared on her head and face. She is a part of some sort of grief workshop, where she has received instruction on how to do this properly. She shows me a card with directions on how to dress. She says, "You know, they're right. I feel invisible!" Even though she would be hard to overlook, since she is sticking out like a sore thumb, she experiences invisibility. Grief, like so much hurt, is often avoided, unseen, and untouched.

As I prepare to say my farewell here at the convent, I have cut out red tissue paper hearts that will be a trail to, and encircle, a bouquet of red roses I'll leave for the sisters as a token of my appreciation for their warmth and hospitality and of my gratitude for my time among them. Here I have allowed myself to turn toward my grief, to touch my wounds, to see my mother and myself more wholly. One of the roses is for me.

❖

JUST OUTSIDE THE FRONT DOORS of the convent is a sculpture of a woman with her arms extended, offering a child. I wonder about the sculpture. It stands with a river of stones at its feet. It would be odd to have here a sculpture of Moses' mother releasing him to the river. The sculpture must be of Mary, but the images I know of Mother and Child always depict her holding her baby close. I spend time looking at the sculpture. Mary is relinquishing her child.

When my son was a baby, he was given a little sailor suit. As a baby, Ben had only the fuzzy beginnings of hair. He looked like the Cracker Jack kid. He looked like he had a prescribed haircut and had become a navy recruit. Being a member of the armed forces is not what I would choose for Ben. Looking at this little sailor toddler, though, I had to imagine that the armed forces just might be in the realm of possibilities Ben might choose for himself. My love for him would have to be so expansive that I could relinquish him to be whoever he would be.

Mary releases her child. When I think about the story, I believe God also releases Jesus, like God releases each of us to be who we will be. No way do I believe that God designed for Jesus to die on a cross. In Jesus being who he would be—speaking and living love—he was killed. After his death, he was released to be everywhere.

Mothers let go of children. Children let go of mothers.

On my last morning walk, I find my eighteenth golf ball, and I am clear on what I want to do. Under the blue sky and the warm sun, I go out onto the grounds of the retreat house and again duck through the opening in the fence just beyond the last station of the cross. I go out onto the wide expanse of rolling hills, and at the peak of one hill, I stand straight and tall and feel the warmth of the sunshine. I pray to open my whole self to all that is good and wise and honest and beautiful:

Spirit of Life, you are present here.

Awaken me now.

I don't want to miss this moment.

This moment is full of power; open my mind so I may
know it.

This moment is full of love; open my heart so I may
feel it.

This moment is full of beauty; open my eyes and ears
so I may let it all in.

This moment is full of meaning; may I fully meet this
moment.

I breathe deeply and feel the breeze in my hair, the sun on
my body, the earth beneath my feet, the spirit of life surrounding me. I have brought my gathered tokens of Mother.
I touch the rose to my head, my forehead, my lips, my heart.
Under a tree whose top branches are sweet with birds, I let
go of each of the tokens. I speak of the meaning I have given
each one and place each on the earth. I say thank you and
strew the petals of the rose like spirits set free.

MUCH CAN CHANGE in eighteen days. I have been at the convent as the seasons are changing from winter to spring.

Suddenly one morning I can smell rain, feel moisture in the air and sprinkles on my skin. Dust is settling with spring rain; the desert sands are blooming roses.

In the beginning, I wanted my forehead touched with ashes to mark my mother's death. Now I have touched my own forehead with rose petals to mark my living. I looked for messages from my mother, and then I created meaning for myself. I walked the hills, acquiring tokens as signs of Mother: a rock, a feather, golf balls, a bird's nest. Then I walked, relinquishing the tokens and her.

The sisters own forty acres of nearby vineyards. They have used vineyards as images for devotional art in their convent and prayer chapel, and little baskets of artificial grapes are set on each table in the dining hall. In their painting of the Mother and Child, Jesus holds a cluster of grapes. Just as Jesus carried forward the teachings of the Hebrew prophets and their works of love, communities are to carry forward the teachings and works of love of Jesus and to be fruitful members of the vineyard. The sisters' vineyard has been hit hard by the sharpshooter virus, which leaves grapes unfit for fruit or wine. It is sad to see withering, dry grapes on the vine.

I am glad to be at a sisters' convent and retreat, surrounded not by images of crucifixes and Jesus but by images of Mary and sisters caring for the sick, the elderly, and the young—sisters washing feet, teaching, singing, lighting candles, celebrating. Eighty-four-year-old Sister Raphael says to me, "Do your work with joy, or don't do it at all."

I believe the followers of Jesus are not meant to dwell on Jesus or his death but rather to lead their lives, perform acts of love, care for one another and others, work with joy, and celebrate. Be fruitful.

I read the following in the book of Wisdom in a Catholic edition of the New American Bible:

> Our body will be ashes and our spirit will be poured abroad like unresisting air. Even our names will be forgotten in time, and no one will recall our deeds. So our life will pass away like the traces of a cloud, and will be dispersed like a mist. . . . Come, therefore, let us enjoy the good things that are real and use the freshness of creation avidly. Let no springtime blossom pass us by; let us crown ourselves with rosebuds ere they wither. Let no meadow be free from our wantonness; everywhere let us leave tokens of our rejoicing. . . . But let our strength be our norm of justice.

I can hear my mother's voice saying, "Barb, get over it; get on with it." I go rejoicing, wanting to live my life, to enjoy the good things that are real and the freshness of creation. I go to leave tokens of rejoicing, to use my mind and heart and strength to bring forth justice and love.

✦

IN THE BEGINNING was the word, and all things came to be through the word. The stories we grow up with shape our understanding of the world. I grew up hearing Jewish and Christian stories in Sunday school. The holidays and holy days of the church were linked with loving memories of family and significant moments of meaning and mystery. When I quit going to church, I threw out the baby with the bath water. At this desert retreat I have drawn the baby out of the water to see what promise it holds.

Biblical stories offer me images to ponder, give meaning and mythic significance to the events of my life, and present metaphors for truth and transformation. As I experience more in life, my experience of the stories also will grow. I have re-formed the stories, reverently playing with them, restoring them to language that opens my heart to their truth.

Since my mother died, a second great-grandchild has been born. She was born five months premature, weighing under two pounds. By the skill and trained care of physicians and nurses, by the attention and love of her parents and family, by prayer, and by grace, this beautiful miracle baby is thriving. Like her great-grandparents, she is strong.

The religious educator Sophia Fahs wrote, "Fathers and mothers—sitting beside their children's cribs feel glory in the sight of a new life beginning. They ask, 'Where and how will this new life end? Or will it ever end?'"

And what about *this* baby, this small story I have been recording and creating? I was compelled to write this story, and now I let the story go. Writing the story has been fruitful for me, and now I hurl the words into the universe and pray.